HOW TO FIX SOUTH AFRICA'S SCHOOLS

HOW TO FIX SOUTH AFRICA'S SCHOOLS

LESSONS FROM SCHOOLS THAT WORK

JONATHAN JANSEN
MOLLY BLANK

BOOK**STORM**

© Text: Jonathan Jansen, Molly Blank
© Workshop guidelines: Dylan Wray
© Photographs: Dispatch Films

ISBN: 978-1-920434-62-5

First edition, first impression 2014
First edition, second impression 2015

Published by Bookstorm (Pty) Limited
PO Box 4532
Northcliff 2115
Johannesburg
South Africa
www.bookstorm.co.za

Schools that Work videos produced by Dispatch Films
www.dispatchfilms.com

Distributed by On the Dot
www.onthedot.co.za

Edited by Wesley Thompson
Proofread by Sean Fraser
Cover design by mr design
Book design by René de Wet
Printed by Creda Communications, Cape Town

The articles on pages 115–127 are reproduced with permission from
Mail & Guardian, where they first appeared.

CONTENTS

WHAT
TO EXPECT FROM
THIS MANUAL

This is not a book. It is a short and simple manual that any community, such as principals, teachers, or parents, can use to "turn around" a dysfunctional or ineffective school. The manual draws on research, the "wisdom of practice" and a good dose of common sense.

There is a lot of published research on what makes schools successful in reaching their goals. Unfortunately most of this research accounts for schools in developed countries and in contexts very different from South Africa. We take what we can from this body of knowledge – for example, that a competent teacher is a critical factor in the learning prospects of children – but also look at the cultures, contexts and constraints within which South African schools function.

We decided to take a unique approach by using film to tell the stories of passion, determination and leadership that are taking place in South African schools. Jonathan Jansen identified 19 successful schools across South Africa and Molly Blank travelled around the country with her camera capturing the stories of what is happening in these schools. These films tell the stories of schools that shift the paradigm and defy our expectations. They are stories of determined and resilient young people who arrive at school at 6 am for mandatory study, stories of teachers who have concrete lesson plans, and committed principals who lead with a philosophy and vision that is deeply felt throughout the school.

As we observe these schools, we focus on what South African schools do, and say they do, in the turbulent contexts of post-apartheid schooling. We call this the "wisdom of practice", the kinds of things resident in the heads and hearts of children, teachers and principals that they draw on to explain what changes their school. These men and women fight and sacrifice for their students because they know what's at stake.

Together, we used what we learnt from these stories to draw out the strategies these schools use so we could share them with you. As you read through the manual, you'll hear both of our voices. You'll also hear from Dylan Wray, who put together the excellent workshops at the end of this manual on how to fix your own school.

Clearly a school in which teachers use the full instructional time available will be more successful than schools that waste the allotted time. A school with high learner attendance and low teacher absenteeism will also do well. We looked, therefore, for the simple things or common sense in drawing out lessons from Schools that Work.

We like the phrase "Schools that Work" (a term used before in studies of schools in this country). It suggests labour, for no school changes without heavy investments of hard work by teachers and school leaders. But it also denotes functionality, the working together of all the elements in a school to ensure a quality education for all learners.

Jonathan Jansen and Molly Blank, 2014

Northern Cape – Kharkams High School

3 RESOURCES | YOU CAN USE TO CHANGE A SCHOOL

The Schools that Work project offers three resources to school leaders (district officials, principals, school management teams, governing bodies and others).

1 | THE INFORMATION IN THIS MANUAL

The first resource is this simple manual, which should be used as a reference; an indication of what the 10 strategies are that can change any struggling school. This is not a checklist and shouldn't be viewed literally. Some of these elements of change will be more important in some schools than in other schools, and the order of implementation will differ from context to context. But we are convinced that in dysfunctional or struggling schools in South Africa, these are the 10 strategies that can change a school.

2 | 19 VIDEOS

The second resource is the 19 videos. We encourage school leaders to bring together teachers or communities or principals of schools to watch these videos, especially those from schools in similar areas, and ask, "What is it that these schools do that we can learn from for our own school?" Compare what you see in the videos to what is written in the manual and work out a plan for change for your own school. These videos are on DVDs in the plastic sleeves on the inside front and back covers of this manual.

3 | UNIVERSITY OF THE FREE STATE WORKSHOPS

The third resource is the University of the Free State (UFS), which commissioned these videos and brought together the principals of these schools for the purposes of building the partnership for Schools that Work. The UFS is raising funds to run workshops around South

Africa to help school leaders implement the 10 strategies for change outlined in this manual. The workshops will demonstrate how to use the material in this book and the workshop guidelines at the end of the book to create positive interventions in schools. For more information on the workshop process visit www.bookstorm.co.za/fix-sa-schools.

Schools that Work will not be able to change all 30 000 schools in South Africa; for that you need a government with the political will, technical expertise and the honesty to acknowledge that we have a serious problem in our schools. But what we can offer is how to change individual schools and clusters of schools slowly and systematically in the hope that this knowledge spreads and the enthusiasm takes root among all struggling schools.

"

South Africa is a beautiful country.

IT'S RICH. But if we neglect

education, we are leading this

country to nowhere. "

Cedric Lidzhade, *Principal, Mbilwi Secondary School, Limpopo*

THE STATE OF EDUCATION

9

FACTS

THE BIG QUESTION

It is the question I am asked most often across the country: **What are we going to do about our schools?** Every South African knows there is something seriously wrong with our schools. And everybody knows that getting our schools right is critical to our future as an economy and as a democracy.

What are the facts?

Eastern Cape – Ethembeni Enrichment Centre

There is this saying,

NEVER JUDGE A BOOK BY ITS COVER.

I would say the same thing.

Let the conditions make them not

judge this school, because what this

school produces is what will

CHANGE THE WORLD.

When they come here, they find love.

When they come here, they find a home.

These teachers are not just teaching

them about what is in the books,

but they also teach them about life.

They build them. **"**

Snegugu Khumalo, *former learner, Mpumelelo Secondary School,*
KwaZulu-Natal

"Sometimes you have a vision, but you feel like you do not know whether you are getting the support. You cannot do everything by yourself. There are grade 11s, up to now this year, they don't have textbooks. Textbooks were delivered to other high schools, but this one, no textbooks. What do you expect then, in your visions, when you don't get support? What else can I do? Nothing. I do my part, but somebody is not doing her part or his part. Our learners are losing a lot. But at the end of the year people will be expecting Mpondombini to perform."

Edward Gabada, **Principal, Mpondombini Secondary School, Eastern Cape**

EDUCATION
FACT #1

Government spends the largest percentage

of the national budget on education.

"The goal is that they mustn't just pass grade 12, they must pass with very good symbols so that they can be able to go and live their dreams. It's not the 100% that makes us proud. What's making us proud is that there's a place for the child in the outside world."

Elbe Malherbe, **Principal, Ethembeni Enrichment Centre, Eastern Cape**

EDUCATION

FACT #2

We spend more money on education,

as a percentage of Gross Domestic Product

(GDP), than any other African country.

"I have the privilege to teach Physical Sciences. I try to show my children what is beyond the wall that surrounds the school. I always say to them, 'It doesn't matter to me at the end of the day if you remember what's an atom or a molecule or remember Newton's laws, but I want to teach you to think critically, to solve problems, and to be analytical in the way you go about it.' I really try to make them understand that this is more about life than chemistry and physics."

Willem du Buisson, **Physical Sciences teacher and Deputy Principal, Louis Botha Technical High School, Free State**

E D U C A T I O N
FACT #3

Despite the large share of public monies going to education, South Africa consistently appears at the bottom of competitive league tables on student achievement.

"To maintain such a high pass rate all the time is not easy. Every year I do bring outside people to talk to them. Last year we had professors from the University of KwaZulu-Natal. When you invite the most educated people in the country it means we are important, so we have to perform like important people."

Mbongeni Mtshali, **Principal, Velabahleke Secondary School, KwaZulu-Natal**

EDUCATION
FACT #4

The education system works for about 20% of our schools; the remaining 80% of schools are marked by low pass rates, few university-level passes and small numbers passing in the gateway subjects of Mathematics and Physical Sciences.

"Some schools want to become so community-orientated that they forget that they must set the standard and the community must attend the standard that the school sets. In dysfunctional schools you'll find it's vice versa. They become just like the community. The school is there to ensure that the community gets uplifted and the way you do that is by educating their children properly."

Owen Bridgens, **Principal, Mondale High School, Western Cape**

EDUCATION
FACT #5

Even though about 20% of high school
graduates qualify for university entry,
about 50% of first-year university students
drop out, in part because of poor school
preparation for university disciplines.

"I have learners who are very gifted. I've also got learners who are in the middle pace. I've also got learners who are in the bottom line. So you see as a teacher I have to strategise as to how to deal with it. Normally I see that there is a group of learners who can't understand what I'm trying to say. I try to make them understand from the level of a learner who has understood me. My intention at the end of the day is to see that a learner has grasped that concept."

Sindhu Mathews, **Physical Sciences teacher, Sol Plaatje Secondary School, North West**

EDUCATION
FACT #6

About 500 000 students, mainly boys, do not complete the cycle of schooling from grades 1 to 12, with dire consequences for social stability.

"There is an increase in the general poor performance of our grade 8 learners. They can't read, they can't count, they can't do multiplication. We are offering extra classes for the grade 8s in Maths and languages to teach them how to write, read, as well as capturing basic mathematical principles. The teachers decided that they've had enough of complaining about the students' poor performance so we offer extra classes for grades 8, 9 and 10 in these subjects."

Verna Jeremiah, **Principal, Heatherdale Secondary School, Free State**

EDUCATION

FACT #7

South African children, on average, receive instruction for only about 40% of their time in classrooms.[1]

1 . 'Introduction' in *Educator Workload Report* of the ELRC, compiled by the HSRC; accessed at http://www.hsrc.ac.za/en/research-data/view/2092; see also Martin Carnoy et al. 2012, *The Low Achievement Trap: Comparing Schooling in Botswana and South Africa,* Cape Town, HSRC Press, p. xvi

"We've got a whole week in the December holidays where the grade 11s come to school and we start with grade 12 work. We actually lay the foundation for grade 12. Our strategy is that we don't let students who fail Maths, and Maths only, in grade 11, go to Maths Literacy. We keep them in Mathematics. We try our best. Every year we've got students who pass all other subjects. But we don't tell them to go to Mathematical Literacy. We let them stay and we work hard with them to pass. And they are also motivated to work hard because their Maths mark really makes a difference".

Anneke Mulligan, **Maths teacher, Batswana Commercial Secondary School, North West**

EDUCATION
FACT #8

The lack of effective early intervention, such as quality preschool education, means that children in privileged schools continue to enjoy a head start over children of the poor.

"Between 2004 and 2006, the matric pass rate was between 34 and 28%. In 2007, we had an increase from 28 to 58%. Then the ball kept rolling. We made a huge jump to 81% and then to 85%. We're striving to convert this school into an exceptional institution. A few years back, you wouldn't have so many people having passed matric. Even those who were passing would go and work in the local industry like factories, supermarkets and restaurants. Now our intention is to produce as many learners who go for tertiary education and who will, at the end of the day, uplift the standard of living at Masiphumelele."

Nelson Ma'Afrika, **Principal, Masiphumelele High School, Western Cape**

EDUCATION
FACT #9

Whether it is Numeracy in the primary grades or Mathematics in the terminal grades, South African children cannot do Mathematics.

WHAT WILL HAPPEN TO SOUTH AFRICA IF WE FAIL TO FIX OUR SCHOOLS?

7

CONSEQUENCES

If we do not fix our schools, and soon, there will be multiple crises facing the future of South Africa.

KwaZulu-Natal – Mpumelelo Secondary School

"The recipe for success is an ongoing process. You have to establish certain things to make sure that [learners] will be successful when they reach grade 12. It's like building a house. You can't put on a good roof if you don't have the walls and the foundation. So we start with them in grade 8, laying a good foundation, making sure first that they master English. Then we emphasise their reading skills. If they can't read, they can't understand, then they can't study. Then also Mathematics. The important thing is that they master the basics so that they can build on it in the higher grades."

Kobus Hendriks, **Principal, Louis Botha Technical High School, Free State**

#1

CONSEQUENCE

The prospects for economic growth

are dim. It is clear from across

the globe that countries that do

well invest in human capital and

this yields both personal as well

as societal benefits in terms of

economic well-being.

"This community is an illiterate community. The unemployment rate is very high; crime rate is very high. Their only hope is education. As the first high school in the area, we want to make sure that we produce better learners to become better citizens so that the whole mirror of this community is changing. We want to change the look of this area. I would like to see this school growing bigger, helping more communities, helping more learners, producing good results consistently, seeing this community changing from poor to well-off families and seeing these learners living a better life."

Bonginkosi Maphanga, **Principal, Mpumelelo Secondary School, KwaZulu-Natal**

#2

The prospects for social stability are slim. We dump tens of thousands of young people, mainly boys, onto the streets without skills and with little chance of further education and training. Crime will increase, prisons will continue to overflow, and the safety and security of citizens will be increasingly compromised.

"For a matriculant, he mustn't think about passing this year, he must think about what he's going to do next year. So if he says he's going to go to university next year then everything else will fall into place this year. He will go to extra classes, he will try to do better and he will spend more time on his exam. But if he has no vision in terms of next year, then everything else falls away."

Owen Bridgens, **Principal, Mondale High School, Western Cape**

3

CONSEQUENCE

The prospects for most high-powered universities as centres of skills development, innovation and competition will be severely hampered. Most universities receive students who barely qualify for higher education, but scrape through on the low system requirements for high school graduation. Those that do make it to university are often unprepared academically and unable to succeed.

"I initially believed that there's this great gap between a school in an urban area and a school in a rural area. But then something that made me change my mind was when we went and did that Moot Court Competition. It was a national competition. Our school came first in the semi-finals and then our school again came first during the finals. And then I realised that, irrespective of where you're coming from, if you work hard you can finally reach where you want, just like we finally did."

Knowledge Dzumba, **grade 12 learner, Thengwe Secondary School, Limpopo**

4

CONSEQUENCE

The social and financial debt of families will increase as high school and university dropouts add to the burden of struggling families. Simply paying back university loans for dropouts will strangle poor households.

"Getting an education is like having a key that's going to open every door for you. Because when I have education, there is nothing that I cannot do. I'm going to change my home, I'm going to turn it into something, a place that is so very beautiful. I'm going to change the world. And I'm not just going to change the world, my community also can be changed and South Africa as a whole."

Andile Makhowana, **grade 12 learner, Mpumelelo Secondary School, KwaZulu-Natal**

5

The inequalities between the middle classes and the poor will become entrenched, and deepen, given that only a small percentage, 20% of schools, are highly functional and the majority of schools are dysfunctional.

"We are from an era where we've been brainwashed into thinking that blacks can do only traditional professions: being a teacher, a lawyer or a nurse. The fact that you are coming from the so-called 'former Model-C schools' doesn't mean that you should be better than my kid who is from so-called 'former black schools'. There is no Model-C university. Once you pass, whether you've passed from a private institution or Sitintile, you're all going to the same university. I always tell them that, 'What you want to achieve in life is all up to you.'"

Rere Tlou, **English teacher, Sitintile Secondary School, Mpumalanga**

6

CONSEQUENCE

While class differentiation will be the deep dividing line between good schools and failing schools – white schools will now include growing numbers of the black middle class – the majority of dysfunctional schools will still serve black learners, so the racial divide in education will continue to deepen.

"The school's motto is 'Avoid the soft option'. We want to teach the children life isn't about second chances. You need to do what you need to do today – because maybe tomorrow there won't be another chance. So 'Avoid the soft option' is don't go for only the easy things: tackle also the difficult things and try and make a success of that."

Elbe Malherbe, **Principal, Ethembeni Enrichment Centre, Eastern Cape**

"It's not only the work in the book. They know that they have to build our characters and they have to mould us to be responsible citizens that will do the best for the country."

Bulumko Sojoka, **grade 11 learner, Ethembeni Enrichment Centre, Eastern Cape**

#7

CONSEQUENCE

The prospects for building a values-based society that holds high regard for honesty, diversity, decency, community and democracy will fracture in a restless, angry and frustrated majority of youth who see no hope.

" If you teach and the learners are not learning anything, then it means you are not teaching. So we started saying,

'WE ARE PRESENT EVERY DAY, BUT ARE WE TEACHING?'

Then someone would say, 'Yes, we are teaching because we are going to class.'

Then we said, 'No, let us interpret it this way:

YOU HAVE TAUGHT IF THE LEARNERS HAVE LEARNT.

But if you teach and the learners cannot

give back what you have been teaching, then

it means you have not taught. Then you must

try to think of another strategy.' **"**

Eudora Nklabathi, *Life Sciences teacher, Masiphumelele High School,*
Western Cape

WHAT ARE WE DOING WRONG?

8 MISTAKES

There are literally hundreds, if not thousands of policies, projects and programmes that aim to change South African schools. All of them have some positive effects on our schools that might explain the marginal increases in achievement scores. But after almost 20 years we remain at the bottom when compared to other developing countries, and most of our schools fail to obtain the marks required in major subjects. In other words, while individual schools or clusters of schools change, systemic change is not happening. So what are we doing wrong?

Gauteng – Tetelo Secondary School

"[Our principal] goes all the way out to instil a group spirit in all the educators. It requires team effort and group consultation. She tries to think what others are thinking, not just her individual thoughts. As a teacher it makes me feel good that my views are taken into account and my opinions are valued. That's the most important thing. You know once you feel that you are important, you are a very key role in decision-making, if you are very significant in the success of a school it makes every teacher feel very proud."

Sindhu Mathews, **Physical Sciences teacher, Sol Plaatje Secondary School, North West**

MISTAKE #1

We overburden schools and teachers with complex policies and demanding curricula when what is required are very simple things such as enough desks, competent teachers and clear timetables.

"I believe in structure. I believe in a definite pattern of doing things. We must start at a certain time, children must know they shouldn't hang around in the hallways; they should be in their classes where they will receive their tuition. Teachers must know, 'I must be in my class. I must be teaching the children. I must educate them; this is why I'm here.' And children must also know they have to study. Everything can only take place if we all strive toward the same goal and this is really to make the school a place where children can learn."

Verna Jeremiah, **Principal, Heatherdale Secondary School, Free State**

MISTAKE #2

We introduce all kinds of innovations and changes into schools, assuming that schools in South Africa are stable environments that can absorb these interventions.

"[When] I came here, the school was hopeless. That year we got 23% in matric. It was not promising at all. To change things was easy because I realised it's not the teachers who are not working, it's the management that is not making them work. Every year we were improving the pass rate by about 10%. I've been trying to get 100% and then in 2012 I got it. My vision is that this school remains on top. That is why I have a slogan that says 'Learners First'. In most cases, they come back, they [say], 'What you did for us was very good because where we are now, we are seen as perfect people because we started from here.'"

Edward Gabada, **Principal, Mpondombini Secondary School, Eastern Cape**

MISTAKE #3

We lack the social will to confront and change the enormous political obstacles – among them the teachers' unions and dysfunctional provinces – to successful interventions in schools. We only engage in short-term crisis management when there is public scandal, rather than responding with solid solutions.

"What [our principal] has done is be open to the ideas that are coming with the educators, coming with the many stakeholders who are responsible for the school. I think that is what has made this school change. He's allowing the educators to invent whatever they want to invent as long as it is going to assist the learners. He has a passion. He wants this school to go further and further. If he's asking you what interventions you are doing and you say, 'I've done everything,' he'll say, 'No, I've not seen that you have done everything. Try some more.'"

Eudora Nklabathi, **Life Sciences teacher, Masiphumelele High School, Western Cape**

MISTAKE #4

We focus on the generic training of teachers when what we should be doing is providing development and support inside the classroom in the real contexts of where and how teachers work.

"Some learners lack the basic skills that they should have acquired even from primary school and now the learner is in grade 10 and we have to bridge the gap. And that becomes a challenge for us because it's like now you are doing a double job. And because we want them to succeed, believe you me, we do these things. We even teach them things that we feel, oh, you were supposed to have learnt this before you came to high school, but we are fixing it now. What can you say? It's all in the line of duty, I guess."

Lulu Nxumalo, **English teacher, Masana Secondary School, Mpumalanga**

MISTAKE #5

We fail to establish *solid foundations for learning* early in the school cycle, with the result that learners in the later grades remain in a constant state of "catch-up" that is exacerbated by policies that demand principals promote failing children to the next grade.

"We've got 1 738 learners. In reality, we are running two schools in one. We have classes where we have 68 learners in a class and it is a challenge, how to go on with teaching and learning in such a big class. But we are not to look back. There might be 68, there might be 70 in that class, but when they reach grade 12, they are going to pass. We are still going to produce the dream that we have and the dream that we will always cherish, to produce 100% pass."

Shumi Shongowe, **Principal, Phumlani Secondary School, Gauteng**

MISTAKE #6

We have become obsessed with pathology, the things that go wrong, failing to recognise that there are powerful examples of schools that work and which offer the seeds of hope for large-scale school renewal in the South African context.

"Our school is situated in a deep rural area. Parents from near and far want to bring their children to this school. Currently we have a total enrolment of 2 221 learners. The enrolment of the school keeps growing because of the reputation that the school has. We find it difficult to refuse, to say we no longer have space, and some parents are finding it very difficult to understand that their children cannot come here. So it becomes a challenge to us as well when we have to refuse some learners admission."

Nkhangweni Nemudzivhadi, **Principal, Thengwe Secondary School, Limpopo**

MISTAKE #7

We invest in often-expensive, small-scale initiatives that deliver predictably good results for small numbers of black and poor students; the problem is that the majority of otherwise-noble interventions remain beyond the reach of most people.

"At Mbilwi we go for quality. Because an ordinary pass, it will not help our children and it won't help our country. But just imagine if we can pass one learner and that learner becomes a doctor in that family. That poor family. Just imagine the salary that will run through that family."

Cedric Lidzhade, **Principal, Mbilwi Secondary School, Limpopo**

MISTAKE #8

We mislead the public with inflated accounts of success when the standard of passing is so low, and the performance of the few good schools conceals the performance of the many bad schools because we only see the average score for all of them.

We give them hope. We give them hope.

WE TRY TO MAKE THE SCHOOL THEIR SECOND HOME.

And that gives them some confidence.

I just can't describe how much the teachers

are doing to make those learners feel

valuable about themselves.

And also the respect that we give to our learners. It makes them feel human. And then it makes them to **KNOW THAT THEY COUNT.** 🙶

Nelson Ma'Afrika, *Principal, Masiphumelele High School, Western Cape*

WHAT DO WE KNOW FROM KNOW FROM RESEARCH AND EXPERIENCE?

7

GOOD PRACTICE LESSONS

There have been several studies on effective schools in South Africa and abroad. We have also learnt much from experience observing good schools over the years.

Free State – Louis Botha HTS

"We are living here and working as a family. We are not just here to teach the children the knowledge, but we are here as counsellors, we are here as their mothers, we are here to assist them. There are so many roles that we play to try and motivate them not to feel that because they are coming from disadvantaged communities they have to carry on this cycle of poverty."

Nobatembu Mpambani, **English teacher, Ethembeni Enrichment Centre, Eastern Cape**

GOOD PRACTICE | LESSON #1

You cannot photocopy change. It is difficult to simply transfer the lessons of good practice from an effective school to a dysfunctional school. Every school is different in terms of the context in which it operates, the culture of the school and the challenges it faces.

"I am not the only person running the school. A school is not a one-man show. Seventy as we are, if we all work as a team, if we all work together, then we are able to do more. If we all dream together, if we all build future plans of this school together, then we see the success of this school."

Nkhangweni Nemudzivhadi, **Principal, Thengwe Secondary School, Limpopo**

LESSON #2

Creating lasting change is difficult. It is possible to "spike" the performance of a dysfunctional school in the short term with quick-fix solutions, but such interventions do not create a school that absorbs and sustains high academic performance over time.

One easy strategy is to hold back weaker learners in grades 10 or 11 so that they do not bring down the average in the external examinations of grade 12. But this will not help these learners or a school in the long run.

"We cannot play down the effect of individual study because it's only then a child realises how much they don't know or how much I know. Then when the teacher comes the next day, the child poses a challenge to the teacher: 'When I studied this and that, I discovered this, but you did not talk about it in class.' You can see that the child is growing. So that establishes a culture of seriousness on the side of the kids themselves. Teachers, when they go to class, they know that they are facing a mammoth task. Something new is developing. You must be always on the alert. You have to maintain this at all times no matter what it takes."

Mbongeni Mtshali, **Principal, Velabahleke Secondary School, KwaZulu-Natal**

| # LESSON #3

Change is not a simple checklist. It is not possible to achieve effective and sustainable school change by ticking off one or two factors in school operations – such as a visible and active principal or a qualified teacher; the way to fix schools is to bring into play a series of strategies (see the 10 key strategies that can change our schools on page 128) that together optimise the chances of turning around a school.

"We need to understand that kids are not tabula rasas. It's not like the educator knows all and the kids know nothing. We build upon what the kids already know. So it's important for me as an educator to understand what the kids already know, the prior knowledge that they have within them. And then building on what they already know. If I approach them as if they are tabula rasas and I know everything, then there will be a problem."

Martin Tinoziva, **Physical Sciences teacher, Mbilwi Secondary School, Limpopo**

| # LESSON #4

Money is not enough. It is possible to have all the material and human resources required and still fail to become an effective school; what is required is the capacity to turn those ample resources (or the resources available) into results – into more and better student learning.

"Discipline should be viewed from an African perspective of a high regard for respect. That's where it stems from. I believe education should produce kids who value their parents, value their past and then focus on what they intend to be, but without neglecting the roots where they come from."

Mbongeni Mtshali, **Principal, Velabahleke Secondary School, KwaZulu-Natal**

LESSON #5

Complexity kills capacity. The more complex the transformation, the more difficult it is to persuade teachers to change. Teachers already face constant demands on their time and complain of mounting administrative paperwork that takes time away from teaching. A good school concentrates on doing simple things well.

"When I enter that gate, I leave all the circumstances of my background behind and I enter with the mentality that I want to learn. That I want to go there and get the education that our parents, mostly, didn't get the privilege to have. This is a uniform of success. People in jail, they are wearing a uniform of regret. So this is a uniform of success."

Sbusiso Mhlanga, **grade 12 learner, Phumlani Secondary School, Gauteng**

LESSON #6

Change is reversible. So many good schools rise but then fall when a good principal is promoted to the district, some stalwart teachers retire or external forces (such as a new and violent gang in the neighbourhood) impact negatively on the school. One characteristic of a really effective school is to instil a sense of "deep change" that shields the school against the inevitable fluctuations in the internal or external environment.

"You really have to appoint academia in the school. I think one of the first mistakes that principals do is that they take whatever staff they come across. We don't do that. There are many occasions we have sent applications back because we didn't feel that a person is qualified enough. The other thing is their attitudes, really. Are they passionate in regard to what they're doing? And secondly, do they believe the children in the community can really do well? If a teacher comes and teaches and he doesn't think the community is going to go anywhere or the children are worthwhile, they're not going to give them the time of day."

Owen Bridgens, **Principal, Mondale High School, Western Cape**

LESSON #7

We know what works – and what does not.
While we cannot simply copy change from
one school and impose it on another, we can
isolate the things that work and which wise
leaders in a school can draw on to steer the
change process.

HOW WE CHOSE OUR SCHOOLS THAT WORK

We decided to look for effective schools that could be models of excellence. We wanted to find schools that do exceptionally well in very challenging circumstances – such as dire poverty, gangster violence, widespread drug abuse, high rates of illiteracy, lack of basic services including water and electricity, broken homes and a high incidence of teenage pregnancy. Why do these schools do well when every other school in the same environment under-performs? In locating the factors that make these schools not only survive but also excel, we thought we might find the seeds of hope for renewal and change in all our disadvantaged schools.

We decided to look at two schools in each province (except for the Western Cape, in which we profiled three Schools that Work). We wanted to capture regional differences so that we can workshop the videos in these regions and refer to schools with environments and difficulties unique to each region.

We wanted to avoid schools that show short-term gains. Rather, we profiled schools that have produced consistently high academic scores in grade 12 over multiple years. We also discounted schools with good results that often come from "managing down" the grade 12 numbers; that is, schools that artificially boost their National Senior Certificate (NSC) results by holding back struggling students in the earlier grades, especially grades 10 and 11.

We obviously wanted to include schools that enable all learners to succeed. Schools with highly exclusive admission policies were also excluded, since such policies often produce predictable results. We generally avoided former white schools since the social and material advantages of history – even with visible changes in the student demography – continue to impact positively on many of these schools. We also avoided independent schools as far as possible since large investments of private funding often create opportunities for change that would not be possible in poor government schools.

Amongst the successful schools that we identified, we also acknowledge that they each have challenges of their own and implement each strategy in different ways and with varied success.

EASTERN CAPE

**ETHEMBENI ENRICHMENT
CENTRE,
PORT ELIZABETH**
Principal: Elbe Malherbe
Learners: 395
Teachers: 18
(1 teacher for every 22 learners)
2012 matric pass rate: 92.7%

"It's not the 100% that makes us proud. What's making us proud is that there's a place for the child in the outside world."

From the outside, the school looks like an Italian villa, with its white columns and red-tiled roofs. It was originally built as a primary school for the children of British settlers around 1854. In more recent times, the building was empty for a few years before it became a school again. Although located in central Port Elizabeth, it draws most of its learners from surrounding townships such as Motherwell. Ethembeni means "place of hope". The motto for Ethembeni Enrichment Centre is "Avoid the soft option" and it is strongly enforced throughout the school. Principal Elbe Malherbe has chosen not to offer morning or afterschool classes because she wants to teach her learners that life is not about second chances and they need to focus while in class. Maths teacher Kathy Bosch runs a dynamic class – beautiful, controlled chaos infused with her passion for the subject. When her students instinctively move into groups for classwork, she encourages it, knowing students often clarify problems for one another. But she also has a hope. "Ooh, I'd love to encourage one of them to be a Maths teacher one day," she said and added, with a smile, "That is not such a terrible job."

MPONDOMBINI SECONDARY SCHOOL, UNAPUNDE, MBIZANA

Principal: Edward Gabada
Learners: 525
Teachers: 17
(1 teacher for every 31 learners)
2012 matric pass rate: 100%

"There's one thing I believe in. A parent sending a learner to the school – there is something in that parent. That parent wants that learner to be educated, although the parent is not educated. So [my job] is to satisfy the parent."

Mpondombini Secondary School is located in a very rural part of the Eastern Cape. Many students live without electricity and water. Cows roam across the road and several dogs often laze in the sun in the school courtyard. Principal Edward Gabada is an example of the power of vigorous leadership. Since he arrived in 2001, the school's matric pass rate has increased from 23% to 100% in 11 years. He has a presence in the school, visiting classrooms and teaching his own Life Sciences class. He hopes the 100% pass rate of his students will show teachers and other students that success is possible. One morning there was a line of parents, aunts and siblings standing outside the staffroom where Gabada sits. They don't have to have appointments; they have all come to discuss concerns about their children. On one day, a mother and her daughter came to explain why the girl had been absent the previous day, the first day of term. Gabada had strong words for the girl and her mother. Then he showed the mother the girl's poor scores for the previous term to emphasise that she needed to help her child and hold her accountable so that she could better her grades. Gabada communicates his mission so clearly that parents don't question his authority; they know he is strict for the benefit of their children.

FREE STATE

HEATHERDALE SECONDARY SCHOOL,
HEIDEDAL

Principal: Verna Jeremiah
Learners: 1 300
Teachers: 48
(1 teacher for every 27 learners)
2012 matric pass rate: 98%

"Discipline is something very close to my heart; to work in a disciplined environment, to enable students to learn well, progress well, achieve. That's possible if children are disciplined. And of course this is something not only the principal can do. I spelt it out to the staff and we worked together to get it to a point where we felt now we could do our work much better. You can't teach, you can't achieve, without discipline."

Heatherdale is located just ten minutes outside of Bloemfontein, but the landscape is very different. Most students at Heatherdale live in extremely poor conditions, many in shacks along dusty roads that are a relatively long walk from school. Many students live in child-headed households because their parents have passed away or have gone elsewhere to look for work. All instruction at the school takes place in Afrikaans. Principal Verna Jeremiah has transformed the school since she arrived, focusing on discipline, partnering with teachers and working actively through afterschool and weekend classes to bring students up to academic standards. Jeremiah has realised that her students come to school unprepared for grade 8 and unable to master the basics of Mathematics and read on grade level. While the matric pass rate is high, teachers acknowledge that within that, the pass rate for Mathematics remains low. Motivation is very important to Jeremiah. Once a week she or one of her deputies can be found in each classroom talking to learners, making sure that they have study plans. As she walked out of one class she encouraged them, "Stay with it."

LOUIS BOTHA TECHNICAL HIGH SCHOOL (HTS), BLOEMFONTEIN

Principal: Kobus Hendriks
Learners: 1 415
Teachers: 63
(1 teacher for every 22 learners)
2012 matric pass rate: 99.8%

"At the beginning I told my teachers, 'If you want to be successful with a learner, you must, and you have to, find ways and means to be loveable. They must love you.' If a learner can love a teacher there's many things that he can do with him. He can accomplish lots of things. But this is where you have to start."

Louis Botha HTS is located in central Bloemfontein. It is a large, old red-brick building and, until 1994, was an Afrikaans boys' high school. Louis Botha has undergone major transformation and has also had to implement new strategies for success as the school has changed. Today the school is almost 100% black and instruction is in English. There is no local suburb that feeds into the school, so many students travel in from the outskirts of Bloemfontein. Louis Botha is also a technical high school. Students can study subjects like Technical Drawing and Mechanics that will lead them to careers in engineering or trade, in addition to the regular academic stream. One unique way Louis Botha inspires learners is through a daily homeroom class where learners reflect on their lives and values. This helps teachers convey to students that they value who they are, and not only how they perform academically. Louis Botha also has a number of learners who compete internationally in athletics. Due to it being a specialised technical school, and due to its successful sports programme, Louis Botha attracts learners from all over South Africa.

GAUTENG

**PHUMLANI SECONDARY
SCHOOL,
KATLEHONG**
Principal: Shumi Shongowe
Learners: 1 738
Teachers: 53
(1 teacher for every 33 learners)
2012 matric pass rate: 94%

*"You become a great man, you become a great man. This profession
is bigger than us. And when those learners are passing, it's like it's your
party every day." – Scara Nkosi, Accounting teacher*

Phumlani Secondary School, outside Johannesburg, was started in
1993 during a very violent time in the township, just as apartheid
was ending. While uniforms are mandatory at almost all schools, the
red and the white of the uniforms here have deep meaning. The red
represents the blood that was spilled when the school was started
and the white represents the hope for the future. And that future
can be seen in the bright eyes of the learners. The 60 students in
Scara Nkosi's Accounting class were curious and, even if their answers
were wrong, they rose their hands enthusiastically. Nkosi's energetic
voice was impossible to ignore. He says that the crowded number
makes him improvise and use different strategies than he might if the
class was smaller. The class was having a complex discussion on topics
like auditing, the economic sector, inventory and fixed assets. The
learning and commitment were echoed at home where Prince Kobedi
and Sbusiso Mhlanga were discussing investment and building stock
portfolios in a community where few people are able to invest and
build stock portfolios themselves.

TETELO SECONDARY SCHOOL, SOWETO

Principal: Linda Molefe
Learners: 1 145
Teachers: 39
(1 teacher for every 29 learners)
2012 matric pass rate: 92.9%

"We have improved over the years. In 2011, we were number one in Soweto with 99.9%. The competition is high. We strive for the best, we put whatever effort and commitment we have to make sure that we get those results. When I attend meetings, you'll find principals asking me, 'How do you do it?' And there's no specific recipe. It's just commitment and starting early to motivate your learners."

Tetelo is located in a middle-class neighbourhood in Soweto, just outside of Johannesburg, but learners come from outside the community, most living in denser and poorer parts of the township. The school has a number of containers to supplement for a lack of classrooms. On a regular morning before school starts students can be found in their classrooms, brooms and mops in hand, cleaning to get ready for the day. Planning is also a critical strategy for Principal Linda Molefe. At the end of the year, he takes his entire team on a two-day retreat to plan for the following year. While things inevitably change, he knows he is prepared. Discipline and parent involvement are critical to Molefe. In the morning, latecomers line up outside the school by grade and give their names so that the school can follow up with parents. One afternoon, during mandatory study time, many learners were sitting at desks outside, since the classrooms were too hot to study in. One group was holding their own dynamic Physical Sciences class under a tree. These motivated learners traded off acting as teacher, using the side of a shipping container as a chalkboard.

KWAZULU-NATAL

MPUMELELO
SECONDARY SCHOOL,
LOSKOP

Principal: Bonginkosi Maphanga
Learners: 761
Teachers: 20
(1 teacher for every 38 learners)
2012 matric pass rate: 94%

"As an educator, as the principal, you listen to the community. What is it they expect from you as a school? As the first high school in the area ... we want to make sure that we produce better learners to become better citizens so that the whole mirror about this community is changing."

Mpumelelo sits in a rural area just on the edge of the uKhahlamba/ Drakensberg mountains. It was started in 2005 as the first school in the area. When the school first opened, it had two classrooms and a large tree that was used as a third. The principal's car served as the school's staffroom. Things have slowly gotten better. Today there are 11 classrooms. However, some leak when it rains, others have up to 100 students, and many learners sit on broken desks or even on the floor. There are only eight toilets for 761 students. In 2010 the school got electricity and in 2012 it got water. Principal Bonginkosi Maphanga doesn't consider these factors a hindrance to success. Regardless of resources or levels of literacy in the community he has always held high expectations of students and teachers, as well as of the school and himself. For several years, the pass rate was 100%, so when they achieved a pass rate of 94% in 2012, Maphanga immediately described the school as underperforming. He is striving to get back to 100%.

VELABAHLEKE SECONDARY SCHOOL, UMLAZI

Principal: Mbongeni Mtshali
Learners: 1 400
Teachers: 47
(1 teacher for every 30 learners)
2012 matric pass rate: 97%

"My vision is to see this school as a beacon of hope when all other schools crumble in whatever way, but Velabahleke remains the hope of the people."

While discipline and commitment are displayed by all principals, at Velabahleke Secondary School, strong and tough discipline is the key to success and that discipline is defined and shown in many ways. Principal Mbongeni Mtshali arrives at 5 am to prepare for his day and then at 6 am he teaches the school's 300 grade 12 students a class on *Romeo and Juliet*. Mtshali has been teaching this class for years. He teaches with a sense of humour and strictness. He is neither a gentle teacher nor a gentle principal, but everything is done for the success of the school. He imbues discipline into the school and both teachers and students feel it. Even at 7 am, during mandatory study time for all students, the school is absolutely silent. Mtshali does not tolerate students who are disruptive or who do not do their work; students who interrupt the instruction of others and his vision of the school. Despite this firmness, his love is felt by everyone in the school. Mtshali's school also succeeds because he is keenly aware of the community he serves and the challenges his learners face. Like several principals, he holds afterschool and morning classes. But he holds these classes for a larger purpose. Many students don't have electricity, space to study at home, or may live in a noisy area. Studying at school gives them a safe space with support from peers and teachers.

LIMPOPO

MBILWI SECONDARY SCHOOL, MBILWI

Principal: Cedric Lidzhade
Learners: 2 283
Teachers: 83
(1 teacher for every 28 learners)
2012 matric pass rate: 99.3%

"Former President Mandela said, 'Education is the only weapon to defeat poverty.' You get a good pass in grade 12, then that good pass is the master key."

Mbilwi Secondary School has been the number one school in Limpopo for several years. In 2012, 325 of the 421 students who took the matric exams qualified for a bachelor's degree. There are seven grade 12 classes that average 70 students per class. In order to meet the academic needs of students, Principal Cedric Lidzhade organises the classes based on ability. In this way he tries to give necessary support to the weakest learners and push the brightest learners further. The commitment and energy of the teachers is a key factor here. Martin Tinoziva's Physical Sciences class is always dynamic and one reason why Mbilwi is so successful. Students solve problems on the board, stand in front of the class and model concepts, and watch as Tinoziva moves up and down the rows as he teaches. His goal is to dispel the myth that Science is a difficult subject and he always tells learners, "There is no right and wrong in science, only mistakes that need to be corrected." In an interview, he said that teaching his students involves more than the content, but also how he looks and acts and what kind of a role model he is as a person, not just an educator. He also deeply respects what his students bring to the classroom. "It's not like the educator knows all and the kids know nothing. It's important for me as an educator to understand the prior knowledge they have within them, and then build on what they already know."

THENGWE SECONDARY SCHOOL, MUTALE

Principal: Nkhangweni Nemudzivhadi
Learners: 2 221
Teachers: 70
(1 teacher for every 32 learners)
2012 matric pass rate: 99.3%

"The vision for the school is provision of public, quality education for all learners, irrespective of where we are."

Thengwe Secondary School is located in deep rural Limpopo. Students arrive on foot, by bicycle, or packed into taxis or on the back of trucks. There is a visual contrast between the rural poverty and the school building. In 2007, when the school had 1 500 students, a new building was built to accommodate only 1 200 learners. Due to the school's good reputation, the difficulty of turning eager parents away and the lack of schools in the area, the school now has 2 221 learners. But these large numbers do not impact its success. The Thengwe debate and moot court team have won national competitions. One afternoon, the team was passionately debating whether rural communities can go green. One student argued that rural communities lack the knowledge to go green while another retorted that rural communities have always been green because of their indigenous knowledge and use of natural resources. At Thengwe, the debate club supplements classroom learning. While it helps students think critically and express themselves, it also gives them pride in themselves and their school.

MPUMALANGA

MASANA SECONDARY SCHOOL, BUSHBUCKRIDGE

Principal: David Masinga

Learners: 915

Teachers: 24

(1 teacher for every 38 learners)

2012 matric pass rate: 94.1%

"The vision of the school is to develop learners in all spheres. We must develop engineers, we must develop business people, we must also have spiritual leaders. So the kind of education that is geared toward achieving that balanced type of a society, to me it is very critical."

Masana's population is economically diverse; some students come from middle-class homes with educated parents and others live in poorer homes. Principal David Masinga operates on a policy of delegation and the deputy principal and teachers take on many responsibilities in the school. Masinga says he always follows up, holds people accountable and also makes an effort to work with staff, students and parents directly. One morning, teacher Rames Sibuyi, standing in front of a crowded grade 12 Business Studies class, asked, "What is the purpose of the Employment Equity Act?" Many hands went up. "To address the historical imbalances of the past," answered one learner named Freedom. "To implement affirmative action," replied another. Sibuyi affirmed these replies: "All of this legislation was designed by the government to make sure certain things are being corrected." In this class, they were talking about policies that their parents, neighbours and they themselves could now benefit from.

SITINTILE SECONDARY SCHOOL, KANYAMAZANE

Principal: Harold Gondwe
Learners: 1 472
Teachers: 52
(1 teacher for every 28 learners)
2012 matric pass rate: 81.6%

"As a principal I need to come up with a vision, but whatever decision I make, I need to get buy-in from the educators. All parents have put their learners into the school so that there will be a difference. So [my role] is to see the best things in the teachers and try to motivate them so that they work with commitment. As a leader I need to work hand in [hand] with parents and educators and learners because at the end of the day we are producing learners who will play a vital role in the community."

Sitintile Secondary School is located in in KaNyamazane, a township not far from Mbombela (formerly Nelspruit). Principal Harold Gondwe leads with a philosophy that the school functions as an essential part of the community. He runs the school with a mandate from parents that the school has a critical role to play in developing young people who will go back into the community and develop it further. He is a principal and a community leader, and some learners also call him *Babe*, father. This is echoed in the school community he creates. Teachers told me that Gondwe has created an environment in which teachers are respected. "He doesn't throw ideas away just because they didn't come through him. He makes us have ownership of whatever we are doing." At a morning assembly, students sang and then, led by History teacher Bongi Gondwe, a united mass of voices loudly pronounced the school's motto, "Unleashing learner potential for global competitiveness." Principals, teachers, and learners have internalised this motto and are working hard to make it a reality.

NORTHERN CAPE

KHARKAMS HIGH SCHOOL, KHARKAMS

Principal: William Hornimaan
Learners: 605 (grades R–12)
Teachers: 20
(1 teacher for every 30 learners)
2012 matric pass rate: 100%

"We give children love. They are part of us and we are part of them … They can go out in the broader South Africa, be the man or the woman they want to be. They can be the president of South Africa. And then they can say, 'I'm coming from Kharkams High School and now I'm the president of South Africa.'"

Kharkams High School is in a small, isolated community. Very few adults in the community are professionals and poverty prevails. The school serves learners from grades R–12, 80% of whom are in grades 7 and above, and instruction is in Afrikaans. Due to the multiple grades, one sees a variety of teaching methods. Students solve questions on blackboards, work in pairs to analyse maps, do finger painting, and play educational games on the grass. Principal William Hornimaan lets teachers do what they need to for student success, and he does what is necessary for his own success. Hornimaan understands he is not perfect and that his staff, particularly those with more experience, have a wealth of wisdom to share with him. In the classroom, and in afterschool and evening classes, the importance of group work is displayed. He, like many educators, believes students can sometimes learn more from each other than they can from teachers. Hornimaan aims to increase opportunities for his learners, and the community as a whole. When children have social or domestic problems, or are ill, the principal and teachers visit these families. Love and caring are inherent parts of the school leadership, facilitated by teachers, learners, the close community and Hornimaan himself.

RIETFONTEIN SECONDARY SCHOOL, MIER

Principal: Willie Julius
Learners: 961 (grades R–12)
Teachers: 33
(1 teacher for every 29 learners)
2012 matric pass rate: 87.8%

"They have that vision of 'I want to get out of these circumstances and the only way to get out of these circumstances is knowledge.' What makes this school special is we are the only high school here and we know that if we are not successful in what we do, we will lose our children." – Gerald Smith, Physical Sciences teacher

Rietfontein Secondary School is in a remote area in the Kalahari just 3 km south of the Namibian border. Afrikaans is the medium of instruction at *Sekondêre Skool Rietfontein*. There isn't another school for almost 300 km, so the school serves grades R to 12. Rietfontein is a very small town and most students live far away from the school and use government-funded buses; some walking several kilometres further. Since the community is so small, principal Willie Julius and his teachers serve as role models to the entire town and, as one teacher said, they have to be aware of their behaviour all the time. Community engagement is a critical aspect of the success of the school. Here there are few other services in the area, so the school fills the gap. Its library serves the entire community, its photocopiers are used to make pamphlets for funerals or other community activities and school space is offered to local churches and youth programmes. Given the uneducated population of the area, it is particularly powerful for the local community to feel they have access to the school. Principal Julius's home visits to talk with parents and check that matric students are studying echo his connection to the community.

NORTH WEST

BATSWANA COMMERCIAL SECONDARY SCHOOL, MAFIKENG

Principal: Else Tsolo
Learners: 1 141
Teachers: 52
(1 teacher for every 22 learners)
2012 matric pass rate: 96.4%

"The failure of one child is one child too many. That one child represents 100% for that family. So I don't see them as a large group, I see them as individuals. So the best that I want for the learners is to behave well, do well at school and pass, go to university. I want the best for all the learners. That is what I spend most of my time doing. I infuse them, I encourage them, I want them to believe in themselves."

Batswana Commercial Secondary School was formerly a teacher training college, so the campus is spread out with long white rows of classrooms and trees and flowers. There is a sense of warmth at the school and commitment despite a lack of resources. The library and laboratory were turned into classrooms and like other schools, there are too few toilets. When I asked Principal Else Tsolo what his priority was, he chose classrooms over toilets – classrooms where learners could continue to strive for the best. Every year he comes up with a different theme. The 2013 theme was *You will never walk alone*. This inspires staff to collaborate. To motivate students, he holds an assembly every morning which includes singing and prayer. One student said that the assembly challenges her and inspires her throughout the day. Here, the principal uses a philosophy of constant encouragement and is a constant presence. In the morning and at break time he can usually be found walking around ringing his bell to move learners to class. He frequently sits in the back of classrooms to observe teachers and students. At first glance, this may not seem concrete enough to be a "strategy", but it is extremely effective.

SOL PLAATJE SECONDARY SCHOOL, MAFIKENG

Principal: Kathirgamayagi Kanagaratnam
Learners: 870
Teachers: 36
(1 teacher for every 24 learners)
2012 matric pass rate: 98.06%

"My vision for this school is to produce a holistic learner. I have a strong belief in producing an academic learner who has leadership qualities and is also able to manage time. So when we talk about managing time, there should be learners who are involved in sports, other extramural activities, and who also have been involved in leadership along with academics. So this is what our mission is."

At Sol Plaatje Secondary School, Principal Kanagaratnam has a unique vision of discipline, which involves engaging students in dialogue about their behaviour and trying to understand them on their level as teenagers. The school is smaller than other Schools that Work and while it charges school fees these are low. It still faces challenges, including learners who are below grade level. One way teachers here combat this issue is by partnering high-achieving and low-achieving students in classroom activities so that they can gain from each other. Excellent teaching is certainly one factor in a school's success. In one English class, grade 9 learners were reciting Shakespeare's sonnet "Let me not to the marriage of true minds". Many made it their own with tone of voice, body, energy, and humour. The teacher affirmed them, allowing the class the space to laugh and clap noisily, and before each student began, the teacher grounded them by saying, "The stage is yours." The grade 9 English teacher's classroom felt different, positive and full of joy, and that wasn't just due to a love of Shakespeare.

WESTERN CAPE

CENTRE OF SCIENCE AND TECHNOLOGY (COSAT), KHAYELITSHA

Principal: Phadiela Cooper
Learners: 396
Teachers: 20
(1 teacher for every 20 learners)
2012 matric pass rate: 100%

"We try to develop a holistic child and we want them also emotionally to believe in themselves and that they can make a difference in their own lives. The way we get students to believe in themselves is by me showing them that I believe in them. And once they start getting the good results for the small tests, then that just motivates them to do better and then they realise, 'I can do this.' But it is hard work to get them to believe in themselves if they have not been given those opportunities elsewhere."

COSAT was started in 2000 to serve as a centre for excellence in Khayelitsha, in contrast to many other schools in the community. The school focuses on Maths and Science, and students must take Maths, Physical Sciences and Information Technology. The small staff is supplemented by volunteer educators, including a Maths teacher from England. In her brightly-coloured classroom, students can be found sitting in groups, using cards, blocks and shapes to understand various mathematical concepts and clearly enjoy learning. The school's partnership with the Science Education Resource Initiative (SERI) has resulted in additional computers and a library. In addition, they assist financially in meeting the social and emotional needs of students in terms of clothes, health and food for their families. Phadiela Cooper runs her school on simple philosophies: kids and teachers in class on time, effective teaching, punctuality, and an emphasis on values including respect, hard work and responsibility. A key to COSAT's success is the way adults inspire students and show their belief in them; in turn, students internalise this and use it to work towards achieving their full potential.

MASIPHUMELELE HIGH SCHOOL, MASIPHUMELELE

Principal: Nelson Ma'Afrika
Learners: 1 187
Teachers: 36
(1 teacher for every 33 learners)
2012 matric pass rate: 85%

"A [principal] is a flexible person who gives support whenever it's needed, be it educators, learners, parents; everybody. A leader with the backbone who applies things in a uniform fashion. Then people tend to respect you. You give them respect; they give it back to you. Then a man who must believe in peace, in creating a conducive environment for learning and teaching so that everybody can work freely in school knowing that they are safe."

Over the last ten years, radical changes have taken place at Masiphumelele High School. Between 2004 and 2012, the matric pass rate rose from 28% to 85%. To effect such immense change, the principal, teachers and the community have had to gather together and consider strategies and policies to shift the school out of failure and into success. Masiphumelele is a small and densely packed township. It was built for 10 000 people, but is now home to 40 000. One thing that makes this school thrive is the openness and exchange that takes place between the principal and the teachers. He gives them space to be creative in their lessons while pushing them to help students succeed. The school also has a uniquely strong relationship with the local district office of the department of education. On one afternoon, teachers, principals and department representatives were sitting in the library, engaged in intense dialogue, discussing strategies for how to support pregnant teenagers and teen mothers and help them stay in school and succeed. For Ma'Afrika, school is a second home.

MONDALE HIGH SCHOOL, MITCHELLS PLAIN

Principal: Owen Bridgens
Learners: 1 300
Teachers: 38
(1 teacher for every 34 learners)
2012 matric pass rate: 95.1%

"What makes successful schools is very unpopular principals and to not always do the popular thing. You can be a friend to everyone and be nice to everyone else, at what cost really? I think as the years go by you learn to be far more subtle, but principals still have to stand on their feet, and many times stand alone. And so if you're not prepared to do that, to make unpopular decisions, that means the school is going to fall."

Mondale High School is located in the very poor community of Mitchells Plain. Mondale has a reputation in the area for its excellence both in academics and in sport, particularly athletics. One teacher described the school's motto as "Discipline, Dedication and Determination". Principal Bridgens runs the school with tight discipline and believes that students must earn his respect. In his Geography classes, Nigel Pelston encouraged his students to read the newspaper and watch the news to understand that Geography is about what is happening around them and not just something in a textbook. Mondale teachers are clearly passionate and if students are falling behind they make an extra effort to follow up by calling parents, bringing students in after school and demanding accountability from learners. In order to get results, Bridgens believes that principals must do a few things. "You must be a disciplinarian. Pride is very important for children, get them to engender pride. And I think 99% is inspiration. You have to spend a lot of time with your children to absolutely convince them of the fact that there's a brighter future there, they're the new generation, they're going to be better than us."

Eastern Cape – Ethembeni Enrichment Centre

5

REFLECTIONS ON VISITING SCHOOLS THAT WORK

REFLECTION #1

THIS IS MY KIND OF SCHOOL – JONATHAN JANSEN

Leicester Road School in Kensington has a plaque on the wall honouring the Queen and her territories. No, this is not a possession of the Crown in West London; it is a Johannesburg school that is one of the most impressive places of learning I have ever experienced.

It is early Monday morning and, after rising at 4 am for the early flight from Bloemfontein, I was not in the mood for small talk. I expect the teachers on their first day back from the holidays to exhibit that semi-depression that we all go through on returning to hard work.

Exactly the opposite; these teachers are bristling with excitement, almost literally jumping for joy.

"Are you people on uppers?" I ask one smiling face after the other as they pass by with their joyful countenances.

There are no children yet, but the place is busy. The principal rushes a few teachers to a management meeting. Others read earnestly from what seems like planning books. Nobody is lazing around, and then the shock: one teacher after another comes to tell me how excited they are about teaching and what a great principal they have as a leader. This is not choreographed; they really mean it. Time to find out why.

The first thing that strikes you is that nobody talks about academic results. The emphasis at Leicester Road is on caring, and the vision and mission statements on the school's website are filled with words of compassion and belonging.

Two teachers tell me with great passion about their love for the children and how hard they work to make every child feel accepted. They raise money to feed hungry children. They employ additional teachers as specialists to guide and counsel troubled children.

The school is basic but clean, efficient and welcoming. The ethic of care is everywhere.

"What is the thing you talk about most on your governance agenda?" I ask the chairwoman of the governing body. "That the children are okay; that the parents are okay; that the teachers are okay." In the cut-throat and competitive focus on academic results, and the threats that teachers and principals are subjected to by the authorities if they do not perform, this school puts care and compassion for their people first. This applies to all.

This is the only school I have visited where the workers also attended my motivational talk and where the staff – teachers and cleaners – appear in one photo in alphabetical order. A small matter, perhaps, but a powerful message that everyone matters in this little oasis in the measurement desert of performance-based education.

Leicester Road is a reminder that we might have gone too far in our obsession with measured results. We might have lost the broader purposes of education to nurture whole human beings with the narrow focus on Annual National Assessment (ANA) results in primary schools and National Senior Certificate (NSC) results in high schools.

Of course, children should do better in Maths, Science and languages, but to what ends? To prepare calculating automatons for the capitalist workplace, or to produce well-balanced citizens for life in a hurting world?

There is a solid body of research that shows that learning is as much an emotional experience as it is a cognitive process.

Children who are loved and cared for generally do much better with the intellectual demands of the classroom than those who come to school neglected at home and bullied on the playground.

Frightened young people, wondering when a slap from a teacher might come for misspelling a word, or scared of punishment that might follow for underperforming in a Maths test, are unlikely to enjoy learning the subject in subsequent years.

Leicester Road restores the humanity that should lie at the heart of education, and is one of the few schools I know that goes against the grain of loveless learning.

As usual, the success of the school lies in its leadership. This is the only school where I am greeted with an almighty hug by the principal and not the formal handshake. Fortunately, black men can't blush.

Renee Abrahams is only the fourth principal in 73 years at Leicester Road and the teachers also tend to form part of a stable personnel tally; after all, who would want to leave this place?

The community around the school has changed as foreigners arrive either as workers or as refugees, but the values of the school remain solid in their embrace of teachers and pupils, workers and parents.

As the teachers begin filing out of the staffroom, the principal reminds them of a borrowed theme to guide them in 2012: "Dream more, learn more, become more."

My kind of school.

REFLECTION #2

SCHOOL TRIUMPHS AGAINST ALL ODDS – MOLLY BLANK

"There is this saying – 'Never judge a book by its cover'," says Snegugu Khumalo, a former pupil at Mpumelelo Secondary School in KwaZulu-Natal. "I would say the same thing. Let the conditions make [people] not judge this school because basically what is inside, what this school produces, is what will change the world."

So what are the conditions that she is referring to?

Nearby stands a beloved tree with a rich history – grade 10s were taught there for two years before more classrooms were built. Principal Bonginkosi Maphanga's Toyota Tazz served as the school's staffroom for many years. And there is a classroom filled to the brim with 98 pupils – better, he says, than last year, when there were 102.

The school was started in 2005 and was the first in the community. Eight years on, staff and pupils would say things are slowly getting better. Today, pupils still share chairs, sit on bricks and blocks, and sometimes squat or sit on the floor.

When it rains, they move around to avoid water dripping onto their books. Pit toilets remain. There are three mobile classrooms, and all are very crowded. Yet Maphanga said he still has to send interested children away, not because of a lack of desks, but due to a lack of floor space.

Grade 12 learner Andile Makhowana doesn't dwell on the conditions at the school because they are not so different from those at home, where he studies by candlelight. He is at the school for his future.

For most pupils and staff at Mpumelelo, which is in Loskop on the edge of the uKhahlamba/Drakensberg mountains, conditions are upsetting but not a hindrance.

I have been in crowded classrooms before, but there is nothing like watching 98 grade 8 pupils quietly listening, raising their hands, following directions – you could almost hear a pin drop.

Back in 2010, when South Africa was hosting the Soccer World Cup, Mpumelelo was celebrating the arrival of electricity – and another year of a 100% matric pass rate.

In 2009, still without electricity, Mpumelelo also managed to achieve a 100% pass rate. The school decided to ask nearby residents who had electricity to help by letting learners into their homes to study together.

Last year, with financial assistance, water arrived. Maphanga no longer had to drive down to the river to fetch buckets of drinking water for the staff and pupils and for the people who cook lunch with food supplied by the National School Nutrition Programme.

One key to Mpumelelo's success is how learners meet expectations. As a former teacher, I have had numerous discussions about how pupils rise to the expectations of teachers. Pupils may say: "I just can't do it." Or, as one teacher in Limpopo told me what one of her learners said: "Just give me a zero, ma'am, because I'll fail anyway." Some expect nothing of themselves and cannot envision a future beyond their dismal situation.

But the power of a teacher conveying faith in a child's abilities cannot be underestimated. To say, "You are capable" and "I will help you get there" can create a previously untapped confidence. Knowing that a teacher has high expectations of their pupils helps many of them to rise to meet those expectations.

Is this any different from our expectations of each other, of our communities and of our schools? Driving up the dirt road to the school, I knew that Mpumelelo was unique. I knew that regardless of how the school and the area around it looked – and I must say it was painful to see – the school was successful.

But if you drove up, would you presume much less? Would you have no expectations whatsoever? If so, this wouldn't be surprising, given the challenges facing so many rural schools in South Africa.

Initially, even the community was sceptical and had few expectations of the school. People couldn't understand how their children could learn with only six teachers, two classrooms and a large tree. But the community was soon convinced.

Nelisiwe Mabaso, whose children went to Mpumelelo, now helps cook lunch for the pupils. "As a parent who is illiterate," says Mabaso, "I am very proud to be associated with this school because through its high standard of education … I feel like my future is bright."

Living in an area with high levels of unemployment, widespread illiteracy and few basic amenities, much of the community, including Maphanga, put their eggs in one basket – the school. Maphanga works tirelessly to imbue high expectations and show the power of an institution to transform a community.

"As an educator, as the principal, you listen to the community. What is it they expect from you as a school?" Maphanga asks. "As the first high school in the area … we want to make sure that we produce better pupils to become better citizens so that the whole mirror about this community is changing."

An English teacher told me that one thing that motivates her is the hope that her learners will have a better life than she has had.

The department of basic education defines underperforming learners as those who receive less than a 35% pass in their matric exams. It is a shockingly low number, and again brings into question the department's expectations of pupils and their communities.

Maphanga's definition of "underperforming" would confound many in the department. Last year, he told me, the school was underperforming because it "only" got a 94.2% pass rate, rather than the 100% of the previous three years. This year, he said, they will be back to 100%. Maphanga, his deputy and a few teachers all have children who attend the school.

"I will change the world, but I was cooked here," said Snegugu Khumalo, who is now a fourth-year Engineering student at the University of KwaZulu-Natal. "The foundation that will make me stand and change the world is the foundation I attained here – in this school that people will take for granted. This school they will say [is] disadvantaged … These teachers are not just teaching them about what is in the books, but they also teach them about life. They build them."

Building them, most pupils would say, to get "the key" to opportunity – an education. But though it is the way out, many pupils expect more of themselves – they want their education to transform their own lives, their families and their communities, just as Maphanga expects.

REFLECTION #3

SCHOOLED IN KALAHARI'S HARD KNOCKS – MOLLY BLANK

I could see the lights of the Namibian border post from the tent camp where we were staying. Each tent had a bed inside, but everything else about the place felt like camping. Our companions were three Afrikaner engineers who shared their braai with us the first night. I was very far from anything I knew.

The drive from Upington to Rietfontein is virtually empty of anything but the occasional animal. After about 280 km, you reach a robot and Rietfontein appears.

The first thing my cameraman Felix Seuffert and I needed was food. So we popped into shop after shop, buying a few things here and there. Four shops later, we found a loaf of bread. I kept wondering where people bought their food. Long trips to Upington every few weeks?

Felix and I really were outsiders – a German and an American who could only say "*Goeie môre*" and "*Baie dankie*" in a town where everyone spoke Afrikaans. We had continual conversations about what we saw and felt, and I couldn't help but wonder what others thought of us after a day and a half.

We had come to visit *Sekondêre Skool Rietfontein*, where Afrikaans is the medium of instruction. This is it for the people here – there isn't another school for almost 300 km. And with an 87.8% matric pass rate in 2012, it is not a bad place to be.

My experience at the school – the teaching, break time, assembly – was much more familiar to me than the town itself. It was the kind of place where you don't need directions because it is made up of about six streets. We even ran into a teacher whom we'd just interviewed at a shop. There are nurses there, but not a doctor.

It is also a place that is rich and beautiful in its landscape – the red dust of the Kalahari – a compelling space to be in and in which to film.

Yvonne Saunderson, an English teacher who attended the school, can't imagine living anywhere else.

"People always wonder, 'Why do you stay there, why do you teach there?'" she says. "Then I say, 'Why not?' Who says I will adapt in another place? I was born here, I grew up here, my husband is a farmer, here in the

Kalahari. I want to be here … The Kalahari, the red dunes, I can't imagine my life without it."

By the time we left, I had come to understand what she meant: people stayed because it was home.

Even people from the education department, those who are responsible for the school, ask these questions.

"The [department's] subject adviser visited from Cape Town," Physical Sciences teacher Gerald Smith told me. "He looked around and asked, 'What is here, what keeps the people here, that this place exists, what do the kids do when they finish matric?'"

It is a question that grade 11 learner Marshall Matthys has been asking himself. He knows the limits of his dreams and those of his classmates. If they pass matric and no bursaries are available to them, then their efforts will seem to be for nothing.

"A lot of the matriculants perform well and finish school, but then they don't get bursaries to continue studies," he says. "Why bother making matric if there is no future? If we struggle, and we won't find jobs? So I'm asking, please, and requesting bursaries for the students of this school."

Like all schools, pupils and teachers alike have dreams for themselves. Teachers want pupils to get tertiary education, to get good jobs and give back to the community, whether they move back here or not.

"They have that vision of, 'I want to get out of these circumstances and the only way to get out is knowledge.' It's these red [school] buildings – that's the only way to get out of here," says Gerald Smith.

At the same time, in a place that is so isolated, and so desperately poor, it is sometimes difficult to convince learners that there is a wider world out there that they have access to. And, on some level, you can't blame them for not believing they don't or won't have a chance for a different life.

The school has 961 learners from grades R to 12 and there are no school fees. About 150 stay in a hostel, but most take buses to school from more rural areas.

We went on one of the buses for the first 10 km, and the land looked empty of anything but dry brush. Some children were dropped off and began walking however many kilometres to their farms. Further on, many children got off at a more formal township.

What is unique about Rietfontein is that the school is literally and figuratively the centre of the community.

"We have pupils from different churches, their parents are from different political parties," says the principal, Willie Julius. "Here are pupils from different levels of the community. Here are children from unemployed parents and children of professional parents. And the school has that uniting role to play."

Where there are few other services in the area, the school fills the gap. Its library is the community library. The photocopy machines are used to make pamphlets for funerals or other activities; the school offers its space to local churches and youth programmes.

Julius is aware of the significance of what the school provides. It is particularly powerful for individuals who may be uneducated to feel they have access to the school.

At the same time, because it is such a small community, teachers are role models, inside and outside the school. In a town where there are few professional people, teachers are seen as leaders in the community, and some said that they must always be aware of their own behaviour.

Julius welcomes the community to his school and he also asks to be welcomed into homes. He makes unscheduled visits to the homes of every matric student. It is an extension of the school's role not only in the community, but also in the home and the family.

"During the preparation for the examination period," he says, "we visit them at home. Firstly, to check if they're busy with schoolwork, because some pupils think the time they [have] at home is for relaxing. [But we know] that, although they're not at school, we are still responsible for them. That's why we take the responsibility to go to their homes. We arrive unannounced and we check if the pupils are busy with examination preparation."

Julius is committed because he knows what the stakes are here. So do his teachers.

"If you were in the Kalahari once and you felt the Kalahari sand, then I believe you just come back," says Gerald Smith. "What makes this school special is we are the only high school here and we know that if we are not successful in what we do, we will lose our children," he says.

But lose them to what?

REFLECTION #4

DISCIPLINE AND DEDICATION PREVAIL – MOLLY BLANK

It's 5 am and we are driving through the gates of Velabahleke Secondary School in Umlazi, about 20 minutes outside Durban. Why 5 am? That's when Principal Mbongeni Mtshali arrives – to read his newspaper, drink his cup of tea for breakfast and prepare for his morning lesson.

At 6 am he makes his way to the school hall where 300 grade 12 learners are packed in, ready to learn more about the star-crossed love of Romeo and Juliet.

Mtshali is neither a gentle teacher nor a gentle principal, but this early-morning class reflects his dogged dedication to his pupils.

He has received a series of questions from pupils and starts the class by reading through the "stupid questions" and calling out the classes that asked them. "Is this 12A? 12B? What were you thinking?"

As the lesson continued, he said something to the effect of: "Even if aliens came down to teach you, you would still fail." Throughout the hour, learners engaged, answered questions and read passages – sincerely happy to be there, even at 6 am.

The key? Discipline. Mtshali says that many learners may initially flinch against such discipline, but in the end they call him a father. The teachers say that he disciplines them. They are always in class on time and teaching.

The word "discipline" is so loaded and is defined by principals in so many different ways. But at this school it dominates in a way I have not seen before.

Mtshali doesn't hesitate to confront pupils, to say that they are "damn wrong" in what they are doing. At the same time, with a hug or a few words, he will heap praise and he recognises the impact of both.

And he has little patience for pupils who do not help him to achieve his goals. Pupils who misbehave or don't do work are, as he often says, "square pegs in round holes", ruining instruction for everyone else. Removing them from class seems to be a simple solution.

This is tough love – discipline with understanding. He has dreams for the future of his 1 400 learners and they thrive under his strict leadership. The matric pass rate in 2012 was 97%.

Mtshali defines himself as "auto-democratic" – an autocrat and a democrat, all in one. He listens, but also has to draw the line. Not an uncaring autocrat, but a firm one who relies on discipline defined in several forms, all his own.

"I carry the vision of the school," he said. "So for me, for that vision to be accomplished there are things that need to be removed on the way."

He runs his school with a purpose and a strong awareness of the community he serves. "My philosophy is that whatever education we have should be based on our cultural influence, so that it becomes meaningful.

"It makes [parents] value kids going to school … It is coupled with a high element of discipline that involves a high element of respect. If education could produce kids who value their parents, value their past, and then focus on what they intend to be – but without actually neglecting their roots – we would be better off."

While he values the community's African roots and firmly believes in parents setting examples for young people, he knows that those examples are often hard to find. Unemployment, illiteracy, poverty and alcoholism take their toll. But amid this devastation the school is valued. It is not vandalised, but respected.

He wants the pupils to value themselves in the same way that the community values the school. While Mtshali holds afterschool and morning classes to help pupils excel, there is a larger purpose; an acknowledgement that many may not have electricity or space to study at home, or may live next to a noisy shebeen.

"My vision," he says, "is to see this school as a beacon of hope when all other schools crumble in whatever way." He knows what the neighbouring schools look like. And that is part of what drives him. He knows that a good education is what will transform the lives of these learners.

One morning, at a school assembly, his style really became apparent. The previous day a parent had come to his office, asking when progress reports were going to be issued.

Mtshali's tone was angry as he chastised pupils for not sharing these reports with their parents. Pupils, he said, have a responsibility to give parents progress reports.

"Your parents may not know what is going on, may be illiterate," he said. "But you shouldn't make them look like a fool to the rest of the world."

In addition to discipline, he relies on another key element – an unwavering belief in his teachers.

"There is no resource that beats a teacher," he replied when I asked him about a lack of resources. "In a teacher there is everything ... A teacher can even improvise where a resource is not available ... As long as they are ... highly inspired to see their kids succeed in life, they will never stop. They move heaven and earth; they move mountains. Teachers are one of the greatest resources of all time."

Economics teacher Nozibusiso Shez affirmed this commitment. "The spirit of teaching – it has to be within you," she said. "That oomph. So maybe that's why he talks about the spirit of teaching. Spirit is something that revolves around you, has to be there with you all the time."

Mtshali references the mammoth task of his teachers, but he has a mammoth task as well – enforcing his code of discipline, trying to engage parents and offering pupils life examples that they may not always get at home. And, of course, aiming to achieve a 100% pass rate.

He tells me that as he finishes each task he proclaims: "Mission accomplished."

So, at the end of our interview, I receive a smile when I state: "Mission accomplished."

REFLECTION #5

AT KHARKAMS, THEY LEARN BY HEART – MOLLY BLANK

Somewhere on the N7 highway, in northern Namaqualand on the road from Cape Town to Namibia, you'll find three towns about 100 km before Springbok. You might not think much of Garies, Kharkams and Kamieskroon. You could actually miss them, driving by. If you do notice them, maybe you'd wonder what it's like to live in such a small town.

"I'm in the middle of nowhere," I wrote in an email to my family in the United States. But, as my father replied, nowhere is always somewhere for someone. And that is very true for the community served by Kharkams High School.

Kharkams is a small and poor community. I'm told that only about 5% of people have jobs. As we turn off the highway, we pass workers tarring a dirt road. It's early and we ask for directions, not realising that if we had driven just a few metres further we would have seen the school. It is the nicest and newest-looking building around and truly the centre of the community.

Six hundred learners from grades R to 12 attend the school every day. In one classroom, we hear mooing and baaing as learners connect animals to the noises they make and, in another, an analysis of Afrikaans poetry. In

this classroom, the pupils are doing basic addition and subtraction; in that one it's higher-level maths calculations, and they are using words such as "coefficient" and "exponent".

I have visited schools with more than 2 200 pupils, but as I spend time at Kharkams, I realise that I have let numbers of learners and overcrowding dominate my thinking as a major challenge schools have to overcome – and am almost starting to believe that if a school is small, it will have a far easier path to success.

Yet here with 600 pupils some classes still have 40 to 50 students, certainly beyond the teacher–learner ratio considered conducive to producing pupils who excel. But excel the pupils at Kharkams do.

Starting the Schools that Work project in 2012, I had a list of topics I wanted to examine:

- Numbers of learners and teachers;
- Exam pass rates;
- Strategies to achieve success;
- The nature of the community where the children live;
- School vision;
- Inspiring learners; and
- Relationships between principals and teachers, and between teachers and learners.

My time at Kharkams refocuses me. Schools don't succeed or fail simply because of a list that can be checked off: they work because of the story and the community they create.

This school is young: it will celebrate its 21st birthday this year. It is the first Afrikaans-medium school I have visited. Though I have filmed in language classes before, not understanding everything that is going on in the classroom is new to me.

Unfortunately I don't have a translator with me for the interviews with teachers and students and I wonder whether I am doing a disservice to them and myself because of this. In my interview with Kharkams's principal, however, we converse in English.

William Hornimaan is a former policeman who, after five years on the force, chose to give back to the community in a different way: he went to university to get his BSc and become a teacher.

"I'm first a teacher and then a principal," says Hornimaan with his big smile. He is warm and gregarious, stern and encouraging. He is a presence.

It seems Hornimaan would rather be anywhere than behind his desk. He teaches Mathematics and Physical Sciences and uses all kinds of methods to engage his classes. Students sit in groups, they solve problems on the board, they do group work and they cluster around a desk as he sits and solves a problem with the whole class. It is unusual to see so many teaching strategies in one room.

In 2012, Kharkams had a 100% pass rate. Parents from up and down the highway want their children to come here. To help make this possible, about 200 students live in a hostel at the school. It is funded largely by the government, and some pupils tell me that living here gives them extended opportunities to work in groups and so support each other academically. It also allows the principal to have evening and weekend classes – he teaches on Sunday evenings.

Like some principals I have met, Hornimaan is not satisfied with the government's definition of academic success. Although the education department suggests schools should start intervention programmes in April, he starts in January. While learners can technically pass to the next grade with only 35%, Hornimaan labels students who pass with 45% or less "intervention learners" and they immediately get extra help. Government standards are not enough for him.

Students come from all over, but Hornimaan strives to involve the community of Kharkams. This is partly because of his unique perception of leadership and partly because of how important the school is to the community.

When he defines leadership, he speaks of his relationship with teachers and learners but then goes further. "I am not supposed to be on a higher level than the poorest of the poor. You must welcome them at your home. You must be welcomed at their home," he says. His home, of course, is the school.

"It doesn't matter, their status in the community. They are people, they are God's people; they are part of this school and part of the school community. You must involve them in every aspect."

He not only involves traditional institutions such as churches and the police department, but also reaches out to individuals. Some community members clean the school and a group of women – who call themselves "Women Against Crime" – provide security. The school doesn't have the funds to pay these people, but he gives them food hampers at the end of each month.

Amid the extra classes, interventions and planning, Hornimaan articulates another strategy. "We give children love. They are part of us and we are part of them."

His dreams for his students often involve leaving Kharkams and achieving big goals. "They can go out to the broader South Africa [and] be the man or the woman they want to be. They can want to be the president of South Africa. And then they can say, 'I'm coming from Kharkams High School and now I'm the president of South Africa.'"

10
KEY | THAT
STRATEGIES | CAN CHANGE
OUR
SCHOOLS

1 Schools establish and maintain
firm routines

2 Schools extend the time for
learning

3 Teachers teach every day and in
every class

4   Students are confronted with high expectations

5   Students are provided with love and discipline

6   Parents are involved in the life of the school

7   Principals are visible in their leadership

8   Principals (and some teachers) are social entrepreneurs

9   Principals act on (manage) the external environment

10   Students are offered a life beyond the school

" What COSAT does is to **DO THE BASICS PROPERLY.** We have the kids in class when they're supposed to be in class, we have the teachers in class when they're supposed to be in class, and

TEACHING AND LEARNING IS HAPPENING

during that time. I think that is the most

important thing.

Phadiela Cooper, *Principal, Centre of Science and Technology (COSAT),*
Western Cape

STRATEGY #1

Schools establish
and maintain firm routines

You know a well-functioning school even before you reach the gate. There are no children drifting outside between classes or youngsters under a tree catching a smoke. You will not find a teacher leaning lazily against the side of the classroom door to catch some sun while engaging in banter with a colleague next door. The playground is spotless and often the security guard at the gate welcomes you warmly with a clipboard. If you approach between periods, you will find neat rows of children walking behind and alongside each other, sometimes in gendered lines, towards the next class period. In a well-organised school with enough classrooms, teachers have their own classrooms, which they can fill with subject-related materials and posters. In other schools, the teachers move between classes and find well-prepared learners waiting for them.

Then as you come closer you hear noise. It is the voice of a spirited teacher rising above the class to pose a question or make a didactic point or remind learners about homework or, occasionally, to crack a joke to break the tension of long periods of concentration. This is good noise, not the more common disruptive or bored noise.

Routines are remarkably similar. The timetable is ready on day one of the school year. The two days before the children arrive are occupied by a demanding schedule involving planning, discussion and review. Parents know what to expect, and that communication between school and home is clear and in advance. Admission decisions are made early.

Teachers teach. Parents govern. The school's senior team leads. Students learn. The sports teachers have a plan for the term, as does the debate teacher, the Arts and Culture teacher and the teacher arranging the Mathematics Olympiads. Roles are clearly defined, and the school leaders keep the team together to form a well-oiled machine of operations.

Homework is a well-established routine. Teachers assign homework regularly, and provide feedback consistently. Homework enriches and extends classroom knowledge, and advances learner outcomes.

Routine is critical to the way that Principal Verna Jeremiah runs Heatherdale Secondary School. Her staff meetings always end at 7.45 am and students and teachers immediately go to class. Once the bell rings, Jeremiah walks around urging students to get to class quickly so that lessons can begin on time. Teachers stand outside their classrooms, showing students they are ready for teaching and getting learners to walk into classes quietly and immediately take out their books. At COSAT, Mondale and Louis Botha, where teachers also each have their own classrooms, students line up outside the class before going in.

Every morning at Batswana Commercial Secondary School, students gather for an assembly outside. The assembly motivates and encourages learners, then the principal rings the bell and students move to class. COSAT has a strong focus on values, including punctuality, respect and academic commitment. They have a system to deal with latecomers, students are taught to respect themselves, their classmates and the school space and incomplete homework is not tolerated. Students know it is a significant thing if they are late for school or class when coming from break. Finally, Mbongeni Mtshali, principal at Velabahleke, firmly believes in organisation and discipline, from his arrival at 5 am to organise the school to his mandatory early-morning classes, to morning assembly and creating firm expectations with teachers and learners of when they are to be in class.

Video examples

Batswana Commercial Secondary
School, North West

COSAT,
Western Cape

Heatherdale Secondary School,
Free State

Louis Botha Technical High School,
Free State

Mondale High School,
Western Cape

Velabahleke Secondary
School, KwaZulu-Natal

"If you are a teacher you are supposed to be an eye opener. So being a teacher means touching lives. It makes me part of those who feel they are molding, building the nation directly. I might not be touching the whole of South Africa but being a teacher means changing lives."

Lulu Nxumalo, **English teacher, Masana Secondary School, Mpumalanga**

STRATEGY #2

Schools extend the time for learning

Only one of the Schools that Work restricts the timetable to official school hours. Schools that Work start early and they finish late. They use school holidays and weekends to embed learning. They hold some children behind for extra classes during any spare time available in the timetable. They send students to learning camps run by any number of agencies from government departments to non-governmental organisations, religious bodies and private companies that offer Mathematics, Science or language classes.

There are good reasons the Schools that Work do this. There is the logic of compensation. Almost every school complains that children coming from the lower grades know less than they should and are below the grade level in which they are enrolled. Teachers constantly feel that they are playing "catch-up" with some or all of the learners. One reason for the extra classes, therefore, is to make up for learning lost elsewhere.

There is the logic of accommodation. The curriculum is crowded. The demands on teachers' time are considerable. Teachers are not only pedagogues but also social workers, health advisers, parent counsellors and more. The department of education requires more paperwork than ever before, which takes teachers away from their first duty, to teach. By stretching the timetable, more teaching and learning time can be accommodated.

Then there is the logic of coercion. Schools are under pressure to perform. The politicians and the bureaucrats regularly visit schools to ensure that barriers to passing are removed. However, for schools that care, this pressure is taken as a challenge rather than as a negative force.

There is the logic of competition. As schools experience success, they are eager to be recognised among parents and the community as a top school. Their names are floated in newspapers and their teachers compete for the National Teaching Awards. They keep a close eye on the previous year's grade 12 results. There is anguish if there are any threats to improvement even for schools with traditionally high pass rates. In places where the school leadership is able to mobilise teachers and parents behind these high expectations for success, the competition functions optimally as a tool for motivation.

At Phumlani Secondary School, Principal Shumi Shongowe uses morning and afternoon classes so that educators are able to move at a slower pace and uplift weaker learners. Then the stronger learners are building on what they already know, which pushes their potential to earn more distinctions and qualify for university. At Sitintile Secondary School, the principal responded to the request of parents and implemented Saturday-morning Mathematics classes for grade 8 and 9 students to strengthen their foundation. Grade 12 students also have morning and afterschool classes every day.

Due to the large number of grade 12 learners, Mbilwi Secondary School has smaller support classes after school with no more than 30 learners. At Thengwe Secondary School, school starts at 6 am or 6.30 am for grade 12 learners, depending on the season, and ends at 5 pm. All other students arrive at 7 am and leave at 4.15 pm so they have at least one extra hour of schooling. Sometimes this is independent study time and sometimes teachers spend the time supplementing what was taught in class or assisting weaker learners.

Video examples

COSAT,
Western Cape

Kharkams High School,
Northern Cape

Mbilwi Secondary School,
Limpopo

Phumlani Secondary School,
Gauteng

Sitintile Secondary School,
Mpumalanga

Thengwe Secondary School,
Limpopo

Velabahleke Secondary School,
KwaZulu-Natal

Many learners at Kharkams stay at the hostel, which enables extra learning time. They have afternoon classes and then group study time in the evenings, as well as weekend classes. Principal William Hornimaan teaches a Sunday-night Maths class.

At Velabahleke, all 300 grade 12 learners are required to arrive at 6 am for an English class taught by the principal. The other students come for mandatory individual study at 7.15 am. All students stay after school for at least an extra hour. Principal Mbongeni Mtshali believes firmly in the power of individual study to strengthen a learner's mind. He also knows that school is often the only quiet place where his learners can study.

Finally, at COSAT, every student is required to attend school on Saturdays. Regular school days end at 4.15 pm. The time is used for personal study, enrichment for advanced learners and individual help time for struggling students.

"You hardly find a time when there are no learners in the school. If you come here on a Sunday, you may find learners being taught. Our morning classes are meant for grade 12 learners. We start at 6 am. We know that their brains are still fresh. They're not yet tired. They can study on their own. We also allow teachers to come and teach them when it is still early. And we find that it helps. We also do afternoon studies. If you are in matric, your school day starts at 6 o'clock in the morning until half past five in the evening."

Nkhangweni Nemudzivhadi, **Principal, Thengwe Secondary School, Limpopo**

STRATEGY #3

Teachers teach every day and in every class

No time is lost in a School that Works. There is a constant buzz down the hallways. Voices of teachers dominate. Teachers are present. In sharp contrast to dysfunctional schools, teacher absenteeism is low. There is a motivational force, even excitement, that seems to draw teachers to their schools and classrooms.

As in any workplace, teachers are absent from time to time due to illness or serious personal obligations. But in Schools that Work there is a plan. The teacher who is absent sends work in advance; learners have to practise the next set of maths problems or work together on a tough Geography examination paper. Nothing is unplanned.

Teachers teaching every day does not mean that the teacher stands in front of the class delivering a lecture for the entire class period. What it means is that every moment in the class period is organised for learning activities that include students working on their own or in groups, students reviewing each other's work, students planning the next day's experiment or students being counselled one-on-one by the teacher over a persistent problem in the particular subject.

Principals in such schools are adept at limiting the influence of external forces on teaching time. Where unions are accommodated, the loss of teaching time due to strikes, for example, is limited, and all time lost is made up immediately through instruction. The constant pressure of workshops and training sessions outside of the school is also carefully managed so that no teacher is away for long, replacement teachers are put in place or carefully planned learner assignments are arranged in advance.

In Schools that Work teachers do not stay away on extended leave because they enjoy working in these attractive learning environments. The school routines and the commitment to success are "pull factors" for teachers in such schools.

Schools realise that their most important resource is the teacher and that while material needs might not be satisfied, there is no lack of commitment in using every minute for teaching and learning.

Ethembeni Enrichment Centre is unique because the principal does not believe in afterschool classes. At Ethembeni, every teacher is teaching when they are supposed to be and students are expected to be focused, so that they don't need any repetition later in the day. Teachers are available for a couple of hours after school if students come to them. Kathy Bosch, who uses board work to get a general sense of the understanding of her class of 60 and group work for students to support each other, says that if one uses teaching time correctly, you won't need afterschool classes. She spends a good deal of class time running up and down rows from desk to desk responding to raised hands. However, during the third and fourth terms, Bosch does have extra Saturday classes for her grade 12 learners. Over 90% of learners show up for the three-hour classes.

At Masiphumelele High School, Principal Nelson Ma'Afrika encourages teachers to try out new strategies for learner success if they feel frustrated. This led teachers to reflect on the quality of their teaching. They decided that just being in the class and teaching was not enough. Teachers have taught if students have learnt and if not, then the teachers must work together to identify other strategies.

At Mondale High School, Geography teacher Nigel Pelston pushes his students out of the textbook and avoids what he calls "old-fashioned parrot teaching". He wants to push students beyond the

Video examples

Batswana Commercial Secondary
School, North West

Ethembeni Enrichment
Centre, Eastern Cape

Louis Botha Technical High School,
Free State

Masiphumelele High School,
Western Cape

Mbilwi Secondary School,
Limpopo

Mondale High School,
Western Cape

Sol Plaatje Secondary School,
North West

textbook and see what they know. This strategy can also been seen in the classrooms at Sol Plaatje, Mbilwi, Batswana and several other Schools that Work. It echoes the belief of one teacher at Mbilwi that classrooms should be "child-centred".

"There is no resource that beats a teacher. In a teacher there is everything. A teacher can even improvise where the resource is not available. They will do anything. They move mountains. They are also highly inspired to see their kids succeed in life. Yes, we do have some limited resources. But more than anything else, the resource that we can rely on is a human resource – my teachers."

Mbongeni Mtshali, **Principal, Velabahleke Secondary School, KwaZulu-Natal**

STRATEGY #4

Students are confronted with high expectations

Within minutes of entering a School that Works you are bombarded with messages of high expectations. The principal speaks to the school and celebrates the 95% pass rate of the previous year. What the children are hearing is that "this is the high standard" and then they hear this: "We are not happy with 95%. We expect you to get 100%; that is our goal for this year." It is very clear from where you sit, as the visitor about to address the full hall or courtyard or in the back of a classroom, that the children are absorbing this message, and that this is not the first time they are hearing it. In fact, they hear this message every day, every week and every month of the school year.

The messages of high expectations are not only communicated through words. Every school has a waiting area that branches off into small passages connecting you to the administrative offices, including the principal's office and the staffroom. The largish waiting area usually has glass cabinets filled with trophies showing success in academics, sports and culture; these celebratory symbols always fill the office of the principal as well.

The names of top matriculants appear on the walls, often with the bright, smiling faces of prefects. Provincial or national awards for excellence in Mathematics and Science Olympiads or in the government's annual teacher awards are visible. A child walking through these passages is confronted all the time with messages of success.

In the best schools, principals channel a majority of their students into Mathematics and, in some cases no student is allowed to do Mathematical Literacy. Maths Lit, in other schools, is a minor option, and this fits perfectly with the culture of the school where high expectations become the organisational norm.

Schools that Work pay careful attention to performance data for the subjects and for the school as a whole in every grade and especially in grade 12. Each teacher sets a goal with their subject department for improvement no matter how successful the subject scores in the previous year.

At Mondale High School, after the June exams, Principal Owen Bridgens posts the names and scores of grade 12 learners in merit order. While someone suggested to him that learners would feel bad if it was made public that they had failed, he knows that this would motivate learners not to fail, and he knows that these lists create competition among students, which motivates them to do better.

Principal Shumi Shongowe of Phumlani Secondary School shows his high expectations every time he addresses a school assembly. At one assembly, he said, "Our school might not be fancy but our pass rates will always be fancy." His personality and expectations echo in the words of every teacher as they encourage students. Students know that their school is special.

At Masana Secondary School, Principal David Masinga holds awards ceremonies to motivate students. He also brings in professionals and successful graduates to inspire learners.

At Schools that Work, there are high expectations of teachers as well. At Sitintile Secondary School, after quarterly exams are written, the subject departments analyse why learners failed. Learners are encouraged to work harder, but it is the teacher who must make significant changes. Each teacher is required to come up with new strategies that they are going to implement to improve student performance, and present these to their departments.

Video examples

Masana Secondary School,
Mpumalanga

Mondale High School,
Western Cape

Phumlani Secondary School,
Gauteng

Sitintile Secondary School,
Mpumalanga

Tetelo Secondary School,
Gauteng

Velabahleke Secondary School,
KwaZulu-Natal

"When you speak to a teacher, they never tell you that you can't do it. Even though you don't believe in yourself, they tell you, 'Don't give up. You can do better.' I remember when I was in my Accounting class and we got our tests back and our heads were down in shame, we weren't proud of our marks, but then our Accounting teacher told us that it's just the beginning and she will help us get through it. And already you can see smiles in everyone's faces, and we felt more inspired to do our best. So I think the teachers are the reason why we keep going."

Nonkululeko Ncokazi, **grade 12 learner, Louis Botha Technical High School, Free State**

STRATEGY # 5

Students are provided with love and discipline

Schools that Work instil a firm but loving discipline among students. All children are required to wear uniforms; and they all do. Girls' hair is neatly cut and tied. No boys have long hair. There is a low tolerance for latecoming. Gates are closed and opened on time, with no concessions for latecomers.

In the course of time, these firm strictures are no longer necessary. Gates in some schools remain open because no one comes late or leaves early. Once discipline is internalised, these schools tend to be less obvious about the controls they apply.

At first glance, these disciplinary measures appear tough and unyielding – until the students express themselves about discipline. Almost everywhere the model of discipline is expressed in one or other form as "tough love". It is understood that the principal or teacher cares for them. Children who transfer from unruly schools find the adjustment difficult, but for once they see that, in the intensity of teaching and the sacrifices made by the school leadership, the discipline rests on a foundation of love and commitment to the students.

The model of care is without bias. All children receive equal attention. In Schools that Work the teachers and principals not only know every child, they know their families and the siblings who passed through the school in earlier years. The care extends beyond the classroom with the school's professional staff demonstrating an active interest in how the children fare in sports or whether the grade 12s handed in their application forms for admission to university. This all-embracing love is the framework within which the discipline applied is understood. The sacrifices of the teachers – coming early and leaving late – translate into a positive response from students when difficulties arise with discipline.

Often this compassion extends beyond the immediate task of the school – such as in the provision of food for hungry children and the raising of bursaries for those who cannot afford to pay the often-modest school fees. Sometimes the families of children are even visited in their homes rather than waiting for children and parents to show up at the school to discuss academic results or disciplinary problems.

At Mpumelelo Secondary School, Principal Bonginkosi Maphanga believes that the key to discipline is to not talk about it on a daily basis. He cultivates discipline by asking older learners to show new ones how to behave in school. At the beginning of the year, the school governing body parents also come to tell learners what is expected of them. This way it is not only the school leadership but also the community and the parents who are telling learners what is expected of them. In that discipline, there is a deep sense of love in this poor school that is conveyed through everyone. Students are supported on every level, always getting much more than academics.

The teachers and principal at Heatherdale Secondary School reach out to the community for various resources to support students. Principal Verna Jeremiah is a strict disciplinarian but she knows that it takes more than academics and discipline for a student to succeed. With donations from the newspaper *Volksblad* and other local organisations, the school is able to purchase new uniforms and shoes for students. On an emotional level, when teachers notice that a student is having difficulties, they are referred to a social worker who comes to the school on Fridays to work with the students. Once a month they have a gathering of parents to help the teachers in working with children. Sometimes teachers also bring in food or clothes to assist students.

For Mbongeni Mtshali, love and discipline are the perfect balance. He gets his grade 12s to school for his English class at 6 am, he removes disruptive learners from classes and he doesn't stand for misbehaviour. He also talks about the power of a kind word to impact a student and their success. One student said she thinks of him as a father figure.

Video examples

Heatherdale Secondary School, Free State

Mpumelelo Secondary School, KwaZulu-Natal

Velabahleke Secondary School, KwaZulu-Natal

Parents are involved
in the life of the school

"I want learners that love their school. I want learners that have dreams for the future. I know that words have power. So I believe what I say to them can create something out of them. I always tell them, 'See yourself as a winner, see yourself as a champion, see yourself as a good teacher.' And words have a prophetic nature. This will come into fruition. It will come into realisation."

Else Tsolo, **Principal, Batswana Commercial Secondary School, North West**

STRATEGY # 6

Parents are involved
in the life of the school

In Schools that Work parents are taken seriously. The parents, first of all, are treated as partners in what the school tries to accomplish. Contrary to the experiences of many poor schools, parents actually do show up and participate in school events despite the inflexible constraints placed on the time of working-class parents.

In most disadvantaged schools parental participation is largely restricted to the official duties of the school governing body. In these schools it is not unusual to see parents on the school grounds offering assistance either in the spiritual lives of children, in fundraising events, in helping the school deal with problems of gangs in the surrounding community, or simply in cooking lunch for the feeding scheme.

Parents are constantly informed by the school about the mission of the school, the results from one year to the next, the needs of the school and more. As the school develops and maintains a reputation for academic excellence, the parents too are lifted by the positive image of the school. Parents queue in long lines, desperate to enrol their children into the star school of the community as they try to abandon dysfunctional schools in the area. Parents are motivated to see the school doing well and to be associated with this success. The myth that poor parents do not have time or skills to contribute are refuted in Schools that Work. Strong principals are also able to engage under-educated parents and guide them in how to participate in their child's education.

Parents also begin to take an active interest in what the children do after school. They know that homework is given and that control over children's time needs to be monitored at home, even if the parent might not be qualified to assist with the intricacies of the subject matter. Strong principals know how to utilise and indeed mobilise positive parental sentiment to ensure the success of both the individual learners and the school as a whole.

In such schools attempts to dislodge the good principal by unions are resisted. Here parents stand up to any external interference in the life of the school whereas in other contexts the school leadership is often vulnerable to such outside forces.

At Phumlani Secondary School, Principal Shumi Shongowe emphasises that just getting parents to show up for a meeting is not enough. It is a school's obligation to teach parents how to be involved, to be clear about what is expected of them. At the beginning of each year, he has a workshop for parents and students, and has created an easy way for parents or grandparents, regardless of their education, to check their children's progress. It involves simple numeric indicators.

"Some of these grannies, they have never been at school … It is your responsibility to try to school them. To say what role you are expecting them to play. And these grannies with the issue of indicators, they also become excited because they can now get involved and give support to their granddaughters and grandsons."

Principal Linda Molefe at Tetelo Secondary School says that his school doesn't function properly without parent involvement. He encourages parents to show interest in their child's education, motivate them and make sure they arrive at school on time.

"We've got a three-legged pot," he says. "Educator, learner and parent. If any of the links or one of the legs is broken, then there is no power in the pot."

Every year, Thengwe Secondary School holds separate meetings for parents at each grade level. They want to be able to talk to parents about their child's education, how to be an involved parent, and what will be required of them and their child during the year in a focused way based on the level of their child, not as a whole school. Parents are held accountable by the school. They have to sign attendance lists and the school calls parents who didn't attend mandatory meetings.

At Mpumelelo and Mpondombini, the principals operate on open-door policies and their availability and awareness of the community is important. Edward Gabada at Mpondombini regularly has a line of parents standing outside his door waiting to talk to him.

Video examples

Mpondombini Secondary School, Eastern Cape

Mpumelelo Secondary School, KwaZulu-Natal

Phumlani Secondary School, Gauteng

Tetelo Secondary School, Gauteng

Thengwe Secondary School, Limpopo

Principals are visible in their
leadership

"You have to see to it that the people you are working with are motivated. We go to the extent of motivating parents to say, 'If you bring your learner here or your child here, you will see that particular person becoming a better citizen.' So as the principal you listen to the community. What is it they expect from you as a school? But the basic thing is that their learners should be taught and it's not just that you teach them to pass, but you teach them so that they progress in life."

Bonginkosi Maphanga, **Principal, Mpumelelo Secondary School, KwaZulu-Natal**

STRATEGY #7

Principals are visible in their leadership

You are unlikely to see the principal of a School that Works tied up all the time inside his or her office. What strikes you immediately about the school leader is visibility. The principal walks around, checks on who is not in the classroom – and why. There is, therefore, a dreaded fear coupled with respect for the giant educator stalking the corridors and the playing fields at any unexpected time of the day.

But the principal does not simply walk around. S/he interacts with the children between periods or during lunch breaks. "Why is your shirt hanging out? Where are your application forms for university? How is your mother? I heard she is not well. I did not like your marks in the last History examination; is there a problem? Are you going to participate in the next Mathematics Olympiad?"

In these walk-around sessions there is a combination of soft discipline and personal interest on display. It is not uncommon to see the principal bending down and picking up litter. The children are watching and this is embarrassing. No surprises therefore that in Schools that Work the school grounds are spotless, whether in a small school or one with more than a thousand learners. This is no accident. The clean school grounds reflect the high standards set for both academics and the overall school environment.

The common problem of absentee principals – due to constant illness or other business interests – is not found in these schools. The principal is present, all the time. When a principal is forced to attend an urgent meeting with the district head, for example, everybody knows where s/he is and the leader returns promptly.

It soon becomes clear that the single most important factor in the success of a school, especially a disadvantaged school, is a principal who is competent but especially visible in the life of a school. In the mouths of teachers, parents and learners, the principal becomes the referential symbol that explains the success of the school – even though it is clear that the head succeeds because of a strong model of distributed leadership across the school as an organisation.

At Velabahleke Secondary School, Principal Mbongeni Mtshali goes around to classrooms every morning to see if all teachers are in class, to make sure teaching and learning is taking place and to check if all students are focused and following instructions. Owen Bridgens at Mondale High School and Else Tsolo at Batswana Commercial Secondary School also have a constant presence, walking around the school during class time and interacting with students during break time on both warm and disciplinary levels. Tsolo even walks around with a small bell to move students to classes in the morning and after break.

Principals William Hornimaan, Edward Gabada and Cedric Lidzhade all teach. Hornimaan would much rather be in the classroom than behind a desk. He uses the class to connect with students in a different way. Gabada uses his students' good results to show his teachers and learners that success is possible. Lidzhade says it is important to teach because then he is leading teachers by example and understands everything that is happening in the school and what teachers are experiencing in class.

Video examples

Batswana Commercial Secondary
School, North West

Kharkams High School,
Northern Cape

Mbilwi Secondary School,
Limpopo

Mondale High School,
Western Cape

Mpondombini Secondary School,
Eastern Cape

Velabahleke Secondary School,
KwaZulu-Natal

Principals (and some teachers)
are social entrepreneurs

"I want to be a teacher, not a principal. I don't want to be sitting in the office. I want to be involved. I love the learners' involvement during my lessons. I love them talking to me; they explain things to me. Our interaction is very good during our class sessions as well as outside the classroom. We enjoy each other, but I'm very strict. I'm comfortable to be with, but I'm very strict."

William Hornimaan, **Principal, Kharkams High School, Northern Cape**

STRATEGY #8

Principals (and some teachers) are social entrepreneurs

In Schools that Work principals think differently about resources. Rather than bemoan, like most school leaders, "the lack of" computer labs or a school hall, or a loudhailer or a library, these principals move from making demands on the department to raising the resources themselves.

The principals scour their immediate environment and determine what kinds of companies or government agencies exist that can assist the school. Rather than limiting themselves to endless correspondence with the district office, they move on their own to identify and recruit resources from the outside.

Sometimes a well-resourced former white school is approached to help with extramural music lessons, a department of public works official may assist in building a netball court or a private accounting firm may fund a computer lab with computers donated by a computer company. The good reputation of the school and the basic business model of the principal impress these companies and agencies, and they are in turn keen to contribute.

And so through a relentless campaign of sourcing external support, the principal gradually builds up the kind of resources that s/he would never be able to raise from the education department. On occasion, the department is impressed with the external support and becomes a partner that matches the funds or contributions made by another party. In fact, many external partners require government involvement.

Parents themselves become part of the resources even if, in poor communities, this simply means participating in the painting of the classrooms over a weekend or accompanying the children on a bus to a sporting competition with another school.

This spirit of entrepreneurship often rubs off on the teachers.

At Thengwe Secondary School in Limpopo, the school governing body has developed partnerships with private companies to fund an additional four teacher posts at the school. These companies also offer educational programmes such as the Eskom Mathematics, Science and Technology Project. The project's goal is to stimulate the teaching and learning of Mathematics and Science, with a focus on the number of girls studying these subjects. Eskom also partners on a project that focuses on strengthening the maths skills of students in deep rural areas.

COSAT has a partnership with and is supported by the Science Education Resource Initiative (SERI). SERI secures bursaries for students, funds for taking students on study camps and support for students who have problems at home, for example students who need food. SERI also funds the school's library, purchases additional textbooks and provides eye testing and glasses to students in need of them.

Owen Bridgens of Mondale High School looked to the community and private institutions to help build his school hall. Mondale is now raising funds to build a good fence around the school. Finally, Masiphumelele High School has developed a relationship with Nestlé, which is building additional classrooms at the school and also funding students to go on learning camps.

Video examples

COSAT,
Western Cape

Heatherdale Secondary School,
Free State

Masiphumelele High School,
Western Cape

Mondale High School,
Western Cape

Thengwe Secondary School,
Limpopo

"The school budget – most of it revolves around the curriculum. So learner and teacher support material, we need to provide for that in abundance. The Saturday class is run by an organisation called Asset. They have tutors who are also educators with a good track record in that particular learning area. Our neighbours here at the Navy also come to school or send their engineers to the school to help learners with Physics and Mathematics and the NGOs are playing a role as well. Because they see the good result of investing at our school."

Nelson Ma'Afrika, **Principal, Masiphumelele High School, Western Cape**

STRATEGY #9

Principals act on (manage) the external environment

What is striking about principals of Schools that Work is how they act as buffers between the school and the external environment. The principal and other school leaders see their role as protecting the school from destabilisation by outside forces so that the teaching and learning programme is not disrupted.

The unions loom large or small in the lives of principals. In areas where the union is very strong, the principal often enters into various kinds of agreements and compromises that shield the school from the worst kinds of interference. This interference is expressed in different ways. For example, unions wanting to push a particular candidate for a vacant position at the school, unions wanting the school to shut down for a protracted strike, unions wanting to protect a member charged with or found guilty of some misconduct, and unions wanting the principal removed for not being a ready ally in the plans of the teacher representative body. Good principals minimise this outside interference.

In violent areas where gangs operate and drug merchants are plenty, the principal also finds ways of minimising the impact on the school. Students are subjected to a firm disciplinary code and find themselves almost daily being exhorted to stay away from such negative influences in their communities. There is a strict set of controls at the gates of such schools and students who fall foul of disciplinary codes are eased out of the school. Expelling an errant learner is difficult, but good principals find ways of managing such potentially negative influences.

As the reputations of these schools develop, the schools adopt more competitive admissions policies, which attract primary school learners with top marks and those without disciplinary records against their names. This is a potent though indirect way of managing the external environment. The students admitted to Schools that Work are therefore less likely to bring in disruptive behaviour from outside the school or to be connected to disruptive elements outside the gates.

At Masiphumelele High School and Velabahleke Secondary School, school is open for extended hours so that students can study at school rather than at home, where there might not be electricity or space for studying, or where there may be violence.

At Rietfontein Secondary School, Principal Willie Julius visits the homes of matric students during the holiday to make sure that they are studying and preparing for exams. Julius is well aware of the home environments of most of his students and is not limited by the traditional boundaries of the role of the school and the principal.

Before Mpumelelo Secondary School got electricity, they partnered with people in homes near the school and asked them to host learner study groups.

Finally, once Principal Kobus Hendriks of Louis Botha Technical High School realised that there was an increased risk of drug and gang activity around the school, he brought in parents for a meeting to discuss how to combat the issue before it became worse.

Video examples

*Louis Botha Technical High School,
Free State*

*Masiphumelele High School,
Western Cape*

*Mpumelelo Secondary School,
KwaZulu-Natal*

*Rietfontein Secondary School,
Northern Cape*

*Velabahleke Secondary School,
KwaZulu-Natal*

"We identify learners that are not performing. We visit them at home and have in-depth talks with the parents. Then during the NSC examination, myself and some colleagues do home visits. We arrive unannounced and we check if the learners are busy with examination preparation. For us it is important to visit the learners at home. We make sure that although they're not at school, we are still responsible for them."

Willie Julius, **Principal, Rietfontein Secondary School, Northern Cape**

STRATEGY #10

Students are offered a life beyond the school

The schools in our study trade in hope. They give children a sense of a world that is larger than the school. Day after day students are not only taught the subjects but also reminded of what they can become. This means that applications to post-school education and training institutions become a major drive in the campaign to show the children that what they see as distant horizons are closer than they think.

One strategy is to bring in marketers from local universities with career advice and application forms. The Life Orientation teacher is not the only one making clear what subjects are required to do Engineering, Science, Medicine, Accounting or Teaching. The process of guiding students into the right careers starts in grade 9 and parents might also be called in to ensure that students make the right choices for the senior grades (10–12).

For poor children, and especially since most of them would be the first in the family to even contemplate university, this elevated offer of life beyond the school brings with it a good dose of motivation. Sometimes those expectations might be exaggerated but the school is clear: given the right guidance and direction, these students have the same opportunities after school as any other child.

Another strategy is to ask alumni of the school who have accomplished careers to come in to address the children. This has a hugely positive effect since the students reason that if that former learner could rise and succeed from the same environment, then surely they can as well.

In a high-energy school the senior learners are even taken on buses to career fairs or to university open days, all in an effort to ensure that the students dream and that their dreams take them beyond the confines of their own circumscribed lives.

Almost every one of the Schools that Work bring in motivational speakers to speak to their students. These include professionals, university professors and former students. Mbongeni Mtshali, principal of Velabahleke Secondary School, feels that when important people come to motivate students it means that the learners are important too. At Thengwe Secondary School, when former students explain how they reached where they are today, students are even more inspired when they hear, "I went here and look where I am now." This interaction with former students makes current students realise that they can have that success as well.

Both Mondale High School and Sol Plaatje Secondary School take students on trips to local universities, sometimes on their open days. These students live near universities but would not likely visit otherwise. Principal Owen Bridgens also makes it clear to all grade 12 students that he expects them to apply to university or college. If he doesn't see applications from them he follows up with students individually to make sure they are taking action.

Cedric Lidzhade, principal of Mbilwi Secondary School, creates a culture of excellence at his school that pushes everyone to excel. The most important thing that motivates his students is the previous year's pass rate. When students see other students passing well and going on to university, they are motivated to do the same. Over 70% of grade 12 students at Mbilwi qualify for a bachelor's degree.

Video examples

Mbilwi Secondary School,
Limpopo

Mondale High School,
Western Cape

Sol Plaatje Secondary School,
North West

Thengwe Secondary School,
Limpopo

Velabahleke Secondary School,
KwaZulu-Natal

"One of our big problems is that very few of our students actually get to higher education. It's an incredible task to give those students self-confidence and to take them on a journey of ambition so that they can believe that they can do it, that life doesn't just end beyond Heatherdale's fence."

Verna Jeremiah, **Principal, Heatherdale Secondary School, Free State**

USING THE VIDEOS FOR CHANGE

Each of the 19 schools in the Schools that Work series has its own story, and each story illuminates strategies that show why these schools are effective.

Like all schools around the country, the Schools that Work have the same goal – to use the power of education to change people's lives and build active citizens of South Africa.

"We want to eradicate poverty in the community that we are serving," says Bonginkosi Maphanga, principal of Mpumelelo Secondary School in KwaZulu-Natal. Maphanga seeks to transform the community by transforming the lives of its youth and empowering them with knowledge and skills that will lead them to greater opportunities and brighter futures.

These videos show how principals like Maphanga are working together with teachers and learners to create a strong school environment that nurtures success. These principals use many different strategies to achieve their missions and they often interpret and implement them in distinctive ways. They also use many similar strategies.

The principals are all strong leaders but they each define leadership differently. "I've studied quite a number of leadership styles but I've never found one that fits me," says Mbongeni Mtshali, principal at Velabahleke Secondary School in KwaZulu-Natal. "There are cases where I set my foot down, but sometimes I have to be highly democratic. I've got to be who I am in terms of what I want to achieve."

"You must set the example every day," says Elbe Malherbe, principal at Ethembeni Enrichment Centre in the Eastern Cape. "In how you talk, in how you walk … in everything that you do. It's to be involved with the children. It's to be involved with their broader family. It's to be involved and see, can you work as a team with the staff? Are we on the same mission and vision with one another?"

As noted earlier in the book, there are 10 key strategies to look for in these videos: firm routines, extended time for learning, strong principal leadership, committed and creative principals and teachers, models of love and discipline, parental and community involvement, a life for learners beyond school, and high expectations. In addition to using these strategies to transform leadership, teaching and learning, it is necessary to think about how these pieces fit together to improve the broader school environment and, in particular, the success of your learners.

- Thengwe Secondary School in Limpopo and Velabahleke Secondary School in KwaZulu-Natal show how morning and afternoon classes provide necessary extra time for study, give learners a space to grow and offer a safe and quiet space for learners who live in crowded townships or without electricity.
- Kharkams High School in the Northern Cape and Mpumelelo Secondary School in KwaZulu-Natal offer excellent examples of parent and community engagement, that support and strengthen the schools. In both cases, the support is reciprocal; the school contributes to the community and the community to the school.
- Sitintile Secondary School in Mpumalanga and Mbilwi Secondary School in Limpopo illustrate the effectiveness of continuous assessment in order to see how learners are progressing over the school year. This is done through informal class tests, more formal tests and also by examining the strategies of teachers to make them more effective in the classroom.

These videos can help you, as a principal, teacher or parent, implement effective strategies to strengthen your school. Here are a few steps to go through to use these videos for effective change.

HOW TO WATCH THE VIDEOS

As you watch these videos, it would be helpful to make a list of the strategies that you see. If you are watching the videos as a group, people may see different keys to success. This will bring more ideas into the conversation. It would be beneficial to watch the videos at least twice to fully understand the lessons and strategies that each video presents.

Some important questions to ask are: What inspires you in these stories? What reflections do you have on your own practice? How would this work in your school? What are these schools doing that you have never tried? How would you reinvent the strategy in your own school environment?

These schools should be viewed as models of success. The strategies are a guide to transforming your school. As the videos show, schools employ the strategies differently depending on leadership styles, the needs of teachers and learners and those of the communities that they serve. Principal Linda Molefe of Tetelo Secondary School in Gauteng emphasised this: "There's no specific recipe of success," he said. "You apply something and try it. If it works for you, you go for it. I wouldn't advise anyone and say we have this particular recipe. No. Proper planning and proper execution of your plan helps you to succeed."

SOME THINGS TO LOOK FOR
- *Each of the 19 schools engages with parents and the community in different ways* – some use parents and community members as volunteers or make the staff available to parents to consult with at all times. For example, Principal Shumi Shongowe of Phumlani Secondary School brings parents in at the beginning of the year for a workshop to show them how to monitor their child's marks and success. William Hornimaan of Kharkams High School uses parent volunteers as safety monitors, cooks and cleaners at the school.
- *Some success factors are more obvious and clearly articulated than others.* For example, Principal Linda Molefe at Tetelo Secondary School speaks directly about the effectiveness of his annual staff

planning retreat. Principal Mbongeni Mtshali at Velabahleke Secondary School speaks about bringing in professors from local universities, professionals and former learners to speak to learners and motivate them. Yet many strategies are shown, but not spoken, and may require deeper reflection on viewing. For example, Edward Gabada, principal at Mpondombini Secondary School, is shown visiting classrooms and engaging with students, but never discusses specifically the importance of having a visible presence at the school.

- *Principals use different strategies to build relationships with teachers and support them.* Many principals use morning staff meetings to create a sense of unity, others make decisions via consensus rather than top-down. Teachers at Sitintile Secondary School in Mpumalanga say that Principal Harold Gondwe is an agent of democracy and gives educators the freedom to do what they think is best for learner success. Principal Kathirgamayagi Kanagaratnam, principal of Sol Plaatje Secondary School in North West, consults her teachers rather than making unilateral decisions. This makes teachers feel valued and creates a sense of teamwork with staff.

- *Learners' energy and investment in their education contributes significantly to the quality of a school as they push themselves and their peers.* Learners don't look only to educators for motivation; they turn to their classmates or inward to themselves. Successful principals nurture learner potential both academically and as human beings. At Thengwe Secondary School, participating in the debate club opens students' minds and teaches them to express their opinions. At Phumlani Secondary School and Ethembeni Enrichment Centre, students are encouraged to study on their own and support their peers academically. These things cannot continuously happen without an atmosphere that encourages a level of independence for learners.

APPLYING THE IDEAS
Examine your own vision and mission

Think about your own vision and mission as if you were a principal. In each video, a principal presents his or her own vision. You need to consider – what is your mission? What is your vision both for your school and for the future of your learners? How would you get the school community and the broader community around the school to go along with this vision and how would you integrate it into the school environment?

Engage in challenging dialogue

In order to get the most out of these videos and maximise their impact on your leadership and school, you must be willing to engage in deep and sometimes challenging dialogue with teachers about the strengths and weaknesses of your school as it is right now. Where are you succeeding and what do you see as your failures? This will set the stage for the next step – going deeper with the videos to see how you want to use these strategies in your school. It could be helpful to consult learners and parents as well to see what other stakeholders think are the major challenges the school is facing or needs to work on.

Implementation

There are some strategies that will be easy to implement fairly quickly and others that need further development. How as a school team will you decide to move forward and create these changes? What roles will people play? How will teachers, learners and parents help to make these changes? On a more basic level, what can you, your teachers and your learners do better and how can you, as a school leader, get them there?

Watching these videos and engaging in dialogue will take you further towards becoming an excellent school. It is not expected that you integrate everything you see and hear in the videos into your school environment and policies. What is critical is to deeply engage in what you see and hear and to have a vibrant dialogue about how to use it effectively. You may connect to one school atmosphere or one school leader more than another. You may choose to implement a strategy using the philosophy of an English teacher at one school instead of a Science teacher at another.

Finally, enjoy these videos. It may be that these stories spark something new and unique that could improve your school and you can channel that inspiration into becoming a more effective school.

TOOLS FOR RUNNING A SCHOOL IMPROVEMENT WORKSHOP

TEMPLATES

5

Workshop design by Dylan Wray (dylan@shikaya.org)

We have developed a range of tools and workshop programmes for groups who wish to run a school improvement programme. You can combine the tools in the way that suits your available time or you can follow the guidelines on page 192.

In this section you will find five templates that you can use while watching the Schools that Work videos. These templates help you to capture key insights from the videos and to focus your viewing so that it is as much a moment of learning as it is no doubt one of inspiration. If you are watching these videos with others – staff, parents, principals or even a group of concerned citizens – these templates serve to focus a discussion after you have finished watching an episode. After watching and completing a template, you can each share how you filled these in, explaining your choices.

If you are running a one-day workshop you can use all of these templates as you watch the various episodes. In a day you can watch at least five episodes, leaving enough time for discussion after watching each.

Feel free to photocopy these templates or adapt them to suit your particular needs. The templates are also available for download from www.bookstorm.co.za/fix-sa-schools.

#1

VIDEO NO. ....

SCHOOL ....

DISCOVERING THE 10 STRATEGIES

10 strategies that can change our schools	Evidence this school is putting the 10 strategies into practice	
1		
2		
3		
4		
5		

10 strategies that can change our schools	Evidence this school is putting the 10 strategies into practice
6	
7	
8	
9	
10	

TEMPLATE

#2

VIDEO NO. ....

SCHOOL ....

DESPITE OUR DIFFERENCES

What is similar	What is different
To your school/the challenges you face/the successes you have achieved	To your school/the challenges you face/the successes you have achieved

#3

VIDEO NO. ....

SCHOOL ....

WORDS OF WISDOM

Words of wisdom/ Quotes from the film	What makes this/these quote(s) stand out for you?	
		PRINCIPAL
		TEACHERS
		LEARNERS

#4

VIDEO NO. ....

SCHOOL ....

COMING BACK TO ME

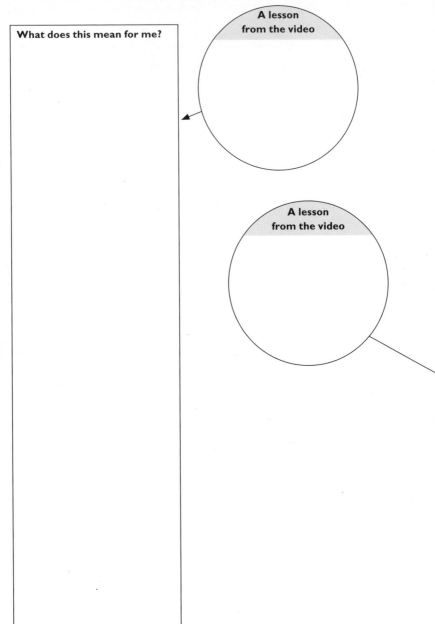

What does this mean for me?

A lesson from the video

A lesson from the video

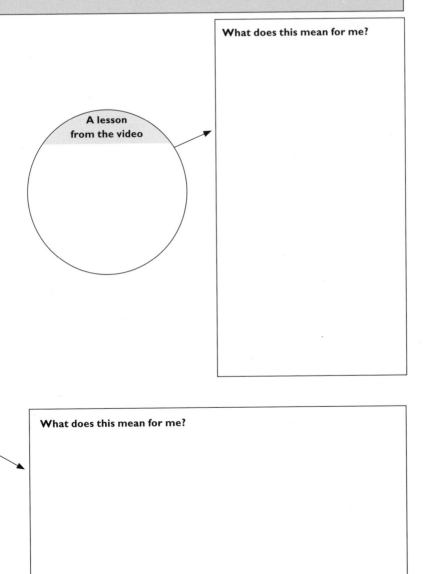

A lesson
from the video

What does this mean for me?

What does this mean for me?

#5 VIDEO NO. ....

SCHOOL ....

FROM LEARNING TO ACTION

10 steps to fixing our school	What are we learning about how we can fix our school?	What does this mean for us at our school?	What are the next steps?
1			
2			
3			
4			
5			

10 steps to fixing our school	What are we learning about how we can fix our school?	What does this mean for us at our school?	What are the next steps?
6			
7			
8			
9			
10			

SCHOOLS THAT TALK

In this section we have provided a number of techniques that help you to have interesting and focused discussions around the videos and/or the manual.

These techniques can be used alongside the templates for one-off viewings or integrated, as we have shown, in a multi-session course.

Watching the videos together as a group of teachers, principals, parents, or better, all together, provides an opportunity to have some important discussions about education in general. But, crucially, it provides an opportunity to talk about your school, your children's education or that of others in your community.

The purpose of these films and manuals is to get us talking and acting. These techniques, hopefully, get the talking going.

Think-pair-share

This discussion technique gives the participants the opportunity to thoughtfully respond to questions in written form and to engage in meaningful dialogues with each other around these issues.

Asking participants to write and discuss ideas with a partner before sharing with the larger group gives them more time to compose their own ideas.

Step 1: Think

- After watching an episode or reading an extract from the manual, ask participants to reflect on a given question, complete a template or write a response in journals.
- This step is done alone.

Step 2: Pair

- Participants pair up and share their responses.

Step 3: Share

- When the group reconvenes, ask pairs to report back on their conversations. Alternatively, you could ask participants to share what their partner said.
- By the end of the activity you will have ensured that everyone has

had an opportunity to reflect on and share their responses aloud, even if not with the larger group.

Talking threes

Step 1
- After watching an episode or reading an extract from the manual, ask participants to reflect on a given question, complete a template or write a response in journals.
- This step is done alone.

Step 2
- Participants get into groups of three.

Step 3
- Participants each share ONE thing from their reflection, templates or journals, moving from one person to another without pausing for discussion.

Step 4
- After the three participants have shared one thing each, the person who started begins the next step.
- They now respond to ONE thing that another group member has shared.

Step 5
- Once all three participants have responded to one thing shared by another group member, the person who started begins the next step.
- They now share ONE final thing. This can be a response to a point made by another group member, another point from their own reflections or a point of clarity.

Step 6
- Allow the groups a few minutes of free discussion where there is no structure to what or how they share.
- At the end of this activity each group member will have shared, listened and responded – ingredients for a great discussion.

Taking a stand

This activity allows participants to share their opinions by lining up along a continuum to represent their point of view. It is especially useful when trying to discuss an issue, such as education, about which participants have a wide range of opinions.

Step 1
- Identify a space in the room where participants can create a line or a U-shape.
- Place "Strongly agree" and "Strongly disagree" signs at opposite ends of the continuum.

Step 2
- Give participants a few minutes to reflect on a prompt or prompts that call for agreement or disagreement with a particular statement.
- For example, you can take a statement made by a principal in one of the videos and ask participants to decide whether they agree or disagree with it.
- Another option is to take some of the "10 key strategies" and use these as the focus for participants to decide whether they agree or disagree with each strategy being an effective solution for fixing schools, or whether they are being done effectively at their own school.

Step 3
- Ask participants to stand on the spot on the line that represents their opinion – telling them that if they stand on either extreme they are absolute in their agreement or disagreement.
- They may also stand anywhere in between the two extremes, depending on how much they do or do not agree with the statement.

Step 4
- Once participants have lined themselves up, ask them to explain why they have chosen to stand where they are standing.
- Encourage them to refer to evidence and examples when defending their stance.
- It is probably best to alternate from one end to the middle to the

other end, rather than allowing too many voices from one stance to dominate. After about three or four viewpoints are heard, ask if anyone wishes to move.

- Encourage participants to keep an open mind; they are allowed to move if someone presents an argument that alters where they want to stand on the line. Run the activity until you feel most or all voices have been heard, making sure that no one person dominates.

Step 5

- To debrief this exercise, ask participants to reflect in their journals about how the activity changed or reinforced their original opinion. Or you can chart the main "Strongly agree" and "Strongly disagree" arguments on the board as a whole-group activity.

FIXING OUR SCHOOL
A multi-session course
In this section you will find a suggested course using the videos and manual. The intention is for the course to be run over five sessions. Ideally, schools will use some of their allocated professional development time to run the course.

Each session focuses on specific videos, specific steps to fix our schools and a specific video-watching template. This is merely a suggested outline to guide a deeper engagement with the videos and manual. Feel free to adapt it to your particular needs and time constraints.

The course revolves around three core activities:
Watching the videos / Reading the manual / Discussing
We encourage you to use the different methods outlined on pages 188–191 so that each session is not a repeat of the previous one. If certain methodologies work better than others for your particular group, we encourage you to repeat those ones.

A suggested learning path for each session
1 • Watch one of the videos
   Use one of the templates for watching videos ▶ (pages 180–187)
2 • Think-pair-share ▶ (page 188)
3 • Read strategy pages ▶ (pages 128–171)
4 • Discussion activity ▶ (pages 188–191)
5 • Watch another video (if time allows)
   Use another template for watching videos ▶ (pages 180–187)
6 • Discussion activity ▶ (pages 188–191)

Session I
Focus
Informal discussions on:
• 8 things we are doing wrong in schools ▶ (pages 54–73)
• 7 good practice lessons ▶ (pages 74–89)

Session 2

Focus
(Following the suggested format on page 192)
Strategy #1:
Schools establish and maintain firm routines ▶ (page 132)

Strategy #2:
Schools extend the time for learning ▶ (page 136)

Strategy #3:
Teachers teach every day and in every class ▶ (page 140)

Related videos
Strategy #1:
Batswana Commercial Secondary School, North West
COSAT, Western Cape
Heatherdale Secondary School, Free State
Louis Botha Technical High School, Free State
Mondale High School, Western Cape
Velabahleke Secondary School, KwaZulu-Natal

Strategy #2:
COSAT, Western Cape
Kharkams High School, Northern Cape
Mbilwi Secondary School, Limpopo
Phumlani Secondary School, Gauteng
Sitintile Secondary School, Mpumalanga
Thengwe Secondary School, Limpopo
Velabahleke Secondary School, KwaZulu-Natal

Strategy #3:
Batswana Commercial Secondary School, North West
Ethembeni Enrichment Centre, Eastern Cape
Louis Botha Technical High School, Free State
Masiphumelele High School, Western Cape
Mbilwi Secondary School, Limpopo
Mondale High School, Western Cape
Sol Plaatje Secondary School, North West

Session 3

Focus

(Following the suggested format on page 192)

Strategy #4:
Students are confronted with high expectations ▶ (page 144)

Strategy #5:
Students are provided with love and discipline ▶ (page 148)

Strategy #6:
Parents are involved in the life of the school ▶ (page 152)

Related videos

Strategy #4:
Masana Secondary School, Mpumalanga
Mondale High School, Western Cape
Phumlani Secondary School, Gauteng
Sitintile Secondary School, Mpumalanga
Tetelo Secondary School, Gauteng
Velabahleke Secondary School, KwaZulu-Natal

Strategy #5:
Heatherdale Secondary School, Free State
Mpumelelo Secondary School, KwaZulu-Natal
Velabahleke Secondary School, KwaZulu-Natal

Strategy #6:
Mpondombini Secondary School, Eastern Cape
Mpumelelo Secondary School, KwaZulu-Natal
Phumlani Secondary School, Gauteng
Tetelo Secondary School, Gauteng
Thengwe Secondary School, Limpopo

Session 4

Focus

(Following the suggested format on page 192)

Strategy #7:
Principals are visible in their leadership ▶ (page 156)

Strategy #8:
Principals (and some teachers) are social entrepreneurs ▶ (page 160)

Strategy #9:
Principals act on (manage) the external environment ▶ (page 164)

Related videos
Strategy #7:
Batswana Commercial Secondary School, North West
Kharkams High School, Northern Cape
Mbilwi Secondary School, Limpopo
Mondale High School, Western Cape
Mpondombini Secondary School, Eastern Cape
Velabahleke Secondary School, KwaZulu-Natal

Strategy #8:
COSAT, Western Cape
Heatherdale Secondary School, Free State
Masiphumelele High School, Western Cape
Mondale High School, Western Cape
Thengwe Secondary School, Limpopo

Strategy #9:
Louis Botha Technical High School, Free State
Masiphumelele High School, Western Cape
Mpumelelo Secondary School, KwaZulu-Natal
Rietfontein Secondary School, Northern Cape
Velabahleke Secondary School, KwaZulu-Natal

Session 5
Focus
(Following the suggested format on page 192)
Strategy #10:
Students are offered a life beyond the school ▶ (page 168)
Related videos
Strategy #10:
Mbilwi Secondary School, Limpopo
Mondale High School, Western Cape
Sol Plaatje Secondary School, North West
Thengwe Secondary School, Limpopo
Velabahleke Secondary School, KwaZulu-Natal

Eastern Cape – Mpondombini Secondary School

ACKNOWLEDGEMENTS

We acknowledge with admiration and appreciation those South African teachers and principals who, against great odds, work to create outstanding Schools that Work, who give disadvantaged children a high-quality education that changes the social and economic fortunes of poor families and communities. We acknowledge their students, whose resilience, investment and commitment to themselves and to pushing one another, all contribute to the quality of their school. One message unified these students – education is the key to the future.

Thank you for allowing us to spend time in your schools and communities, and for so honestly sharing your stories, your challenges and your hopes.

We also want to deeply thank the committed team of people who worked on the Schools that Work videos over the last year and a half. Alex Ford-Robertson, Bart Love and Felix Seuffert journeyed across South Africa, capturing the country in all its beauty. Leasha Love and Anna Telford helped to take what we filmed and edit it into the stories that you see; Daniel Eppel's music took all our work to another level; Andy Wonnacott helped put it all together. Thank you for your collaboration and for going on this journey with us. We could not have done it without you.

And finally, this book owes its quality and depth to the editorial guidance and leadership of Louise Grantham, one of the best in the business, and the creative mind and courage of editorial manager, Russell Clarke, who shepherded the work to completion; to Louise and Russell our heartfelt thanks for making a rough work in the field appear so beautifully in print.

INDEX